TREASURES,
SHIPWRECKS
AND THE DAWN OF
RED SEA DIVING

A Pioneer's Journey

Howard Rosenstein

ISBN 978-1-909455-53-5 (Hardback)

Cataloguing-In-Publication Data.
A catalogue record for this book can be
obtained from the British Library.

Cover Design © 2024 Dived Up.
Diver photo © David Doubilet.

Printed in Malta.

Published 2024 by

DIVED UP

Dived Up Publications
Bournemouth • United Kingdom
Email info@divedup.com
Web DivedUp.com

To my wife, Sharon, without you, there wouldn't have
been anything as interesting to write about.

And to our beautiful children, Ayelet, Nadav, Daria and Ariel.

And to all those wonderful friends who helped me along the way.
You know who you are.

Contents

Publisher's note

The views and opinions in this book are those of the author and not necessarily shared by the publisher. The text is based on the author's knowledge, experience and expertise concerning which the publisher cannot accept responsibility. Readers should draw their own conclusions concerning the possibility of alternative views, accounts, descriptions or explanations.

Many of the images in this book are from the author's personal archive, with some over fifty years old. Where necessary, they have been restored and/or edited, although they remain true to the subjects and situations they were taken in. In other cases little could be done and he asks for your understanding if a low quality but important photograph has been included.

The book uses American English, in keeping with the original manuscript, with some international quirks in keeping with his colorful life.

About the author

Howard Rosenstein.

Howard Rosenstein is an original. He overcame all manner of political machinations to pioneer diving tourism in the Red Sea, whilst simultaneously lobbying for and achieving protections for a globally important, yet fragile marine ecosystem. He did this first from the shores of Sinai, then from live-aboard dive boats, taking them as far as the Aldabra Atoll, Seychelles. Later, with his son Nadav, he pivoted his Fantasea brand to become a success in the underwater photography market. Howard was inducted into the International Scuba Diving Hall of Fame in 2009. In this memoir, he finally shares some of his more surprising as well as favorite stories from the earlier part of his fifty-year plus diving career.

Foreword by Sylvia Earle

Oceanographer, National Geographic Explorer, Founder of Mission Blue.

Once in a great while, a book appears that combines masterful story-telling, riveting adventure, charismatic characters, and meaningful messages that will haunt you long after the final page is turned. For me, *Treasures, Shipwrecks & the Dawn of Red Sea Diving* is that book...

Here are swashbuckling sea stories, shipwrecks galore, and the chance discovery of a treasure-trove of ancient gold coins. But the true treasure and enduring appeal of this book is the personal journey of the author, Howard Rosenstein, a legendary ocean explorer, gifted photographer and successful entrepreneur but also a witness and active participant in some of the most extraordinary moments in the recent history of the conflicted countries that surround the Red Sea. Rosenstein's reflections on the cost of war — and peace — imposed on people and the places they hold dear are profoundly personal and deeply moving.

I thought I knew something about Howard Rosenstein, well known for his pioneering ventures that first brought global attention to the exceptional nature of the Red Sea as a top destination for divers including diving scientists. I devoured the many accounts in the *National Geographic* magazine that he shared with the esteemed "Shark Lady," Eugenie Clark, and renowned photographer, David Doubilet, whom he enticed to join him in "paradise." I even had an opportunity to witness the author in action, underwater, during a memorable shared dive. But as I immersed myself in this book, I was mesmerized as I learned how Rosenstein, starting with little more than a dream, uncanny resourcefulness, sharp wit and unfailing sense of humor, created a highly successful enterprise that transformed awareness of the Red Sea from a place on a map into recognition as one of the greatest wonders of the world, underwater and above.

Abandoning the atmosphere above and dissolving into liquid space frees mind and soul with a keen sense of being among galaxies of creatures who neither know nor care whether you are a CEO, acclaimed musician, noted scientist, leader of a country or a teenager on vacation.

Sea creatures may not care about us, but in recent decades, it has become increasingly urgent that we care about them.

Since Rosenstein first glimpsed the pristine grandeur of coral reefs and the astonishing abundance of life in the Red Sea, coral reefs globally have been reduced by half. Ninety percent of the sharks worldwide are gone and everywhere, pole to pole, populations of fish and other ocean wildlife have declined sharply owing to industrial-scale fishing. Since the 1970s, the ocean has become awash with plastic trash and other wastes. At the same time, the ocean has become recognized as the living blue engine that drives planetary temperature, chemistry, climate and weather, and embraces 97 percent of the biosphere. If the ocean is in trouble, so are we. It is and we are.

Bravo, Howard Rosenstein for your role in securing protection for some of the Red Sea's iconic places and for inspiring more than one generation to understand why taking care of the ocean means taking care of life itself. I urge readers to dive into this book for vicarious adventure, for insight into a life well lived, for reasons why you, too, should succumb to the urge to submerge, and for unbelievable stories that are most wonderful because they are true.

Sylvia Earle with the author. PHOTO: ITAMAR GRINBERG

Foreword by David Doubilet

World-renowned underwater photographer.

Sinai for many is an arid, earthen expanse that shimmers in the unrelenting glare of the sun. It is the biblical center for mankind and the birthplace of western civilization. For Howard Rosenstein, this wedge of ancient sand caressed by the blue fingers of the northern end of the Red Sea was like an ancient ship, permanently at anchor in a vast unexplored coral garden.

Treasures, Shipwrecks and the Dawn of Red Sea Diving reveals a Howard unknown to me, the parts of his life we never got to talk about sitting on a dive boat. I learned he was the best kind of authentic adventurer: wandering to corners of the world that owned his curiosity. He was not content with the promise of California that so many seek, but sought the challenges in life that you have to reach for mentally, emotionally, financially and physically — challenges that make you aware you are alive every day. The Red Sea was a dream that would unfold its secrets to him. When the glint of the Mediterranean beckoned him in the millennia-old harbor of Caesarea, he submerged on snorkel peering into a world eyes had never seen. He was rewarded with gold, but the true wealth came from his discovery of precious living jewels, the Red Sea reefs.

Howard and Sharon forged their future in the sea, opening Red Sea Divers on a two-mile-long crescent of yellow sand in Na'ama Bay, Sharm El Sheikh, using a World War I boxcar as headquarters. It was unseen, remote ocean and it was seductive to scientists like Dr. Eugenie Clark, researchers from Hebrew University, divers, photographers, filmmakers, writers, poets and musicians.

These reefs were a living laboratory for Dr. Clark, an ichthyologist, University of Maryland professor and National Geographic Society grantee. We became an underwater team: She the scientist, me the visual storyteller. The Red Sea was my underwater studio, every dive a voyage of discovery. Red Sea Divers became our compass, guiding us through a decade plus of stories. We shared this coral kingdom — the creatures, newly discovered species and behaviors — with the world on the pages of *National Geographic*. Howard Rosenstein had a dream that he made a reality — he built, and they came. It was a coral Camelot.

The author diving
at Ras Mohammed.
PHOTO: DAVID DOUBILET

En route, passing the Azores on *MV Arad*.

Introduction

So, there I was, like millions of others, at home, marooned by Covid. After five decades at sea — or, more often, under it — I felt like a fish out of water. Sitting at my computer, clicking through thousands of photos, I relived my adventures and realized what better time than now to take up the suggestion of friends and family to write a book. Aside from being a diver, teacher and entrepreneur, I'm a storyteller at heart.

What you will find here is not a definitive account of my career — I wouldn't want to put you through that ordeal — but a collection of stand-out stories from the early years. Most occur in Sinai, where I helped establish the diving industry while the peninsula was under Israeli rule. When I first arrived in Sharm El Sheikh, it was a ramshackle outpost without a neon sign in sight. Over a decade my partners and I built a flourishing diving center that attracted an international clientele. Ironically, it was peace — something so lacking in our world today — that ended our enterprise: The Egypt-Israel peace treaty. But before plunging into my Israeli life, I should take you back sixty-five years to a place 7,500 miles away.

I launched my career in the water business at age eleven. My family was living in West Hollywood, California, having moved there from Brooklyn when I was still a toddler. Equipped with a bucket, sponge and liquid soap, I would knock on the door of any neighbor who had a dirty car in their driveway. Among my customers was an actress whose show business career began forty years prior to our meeting, as a Goldwyn Girl. After I finished cleaning her car, she sat me down for a cup of lemonade. She would tell me stories about the early days of Hollywood. One day, she surprised me with a prophecy. "Howie," she said, "when you grow up, you will be a world traveler." This was something that could not have been farther from my mind as a sixth grader. When I asked her how she arrived at that prediction she surprised me again. She looked me in the eye and said, "Because you have a space between your front teeth."

Perhaps she was some kind of oral oracle. Within seven years, I started traveling the world, and it seems like I have never stopped — even after the gap in my teeth closed.

My journey began in 1966 after I finished a year of community college. My cousin Marc and I obtained passage on an Israeli freighter headed from Beaumont, Texas, to Haifa, Israel. In return for a free trip, we were assigned menial tasks throughout the twenty-day voyage, primarily chipping and applying anti-rust paint wherever needed on the Israeli ship *MV Arad*, a forty-thousand-ton general cargo vessel. It was tedious, but we loved every minute of the adventure. Once we docked in Haifa port, we hitchhiked our way throughout Israel, ending up at the southernmost town of Eilat on the Red Sea. With a borrowed mask, I put my head underwater and was blown away by the tropical fish and beautiful corals.

I would have stayed, but I had to return to the States to finish my degree in anthropology before I could return to Israel. However, my timetable was upset the following spring. With war looming for Israel, I volunteered to serve in the army or in some other capacity. It was one of survival for our people. Just as I was preparing to leave, fighting broke out and Israel was closed to civilian flights. By the time it ended, with Israel's stunning victory in six days, the nation no longer urgently needed volunteers.

Just a year later, in 1968, I received a full scholarship to study in the Overseas Students program at Tel Aviv University. And that is when this memoir begins. In vignettes, anecdotes and photos I recount how I got in on the diving industry and developed a business that spanned from the Mediterranean to the Indian Ocean. My career introduced me to the pioneers of underwater exploration and such wide-ranging figures as a maestro and a moonwalker, best-selling authors and prize-winning photographers, international celebrities and slippery fugitives. It took me inside the murky bowels of shipwrecks, up close with amorous sharks, and into tangles with both Egyptian and Israeli soldiers. I was most proud to have played a small part in the historic peace process between Israel and Egypt, which, once completed, forced me to restart my life.

As much as I have relied on correspondence, newspaper and magazine clippings, and my pal Google to backstop my memory, I have reconstructed conversations to the best of my knowledge. If I have gone off course, I welcome readers to let me know.

Enough said for now. Feel free to dive right in.

Mediterranean Sea

• Tel-Aviv

Israel

SINAI

Eilat •
• Aqaba

Nuweiba •

Gulf of Suez

Dahab •

Gulf of Aqaba

Egypt

Saudi
Arabia

Sharm
El Sheikh •

Tiran
island

Ras
Mohammed

Shadwan
island

Satellite image of the
Sinai Peninsular and
Red Sea. PHOTO: NASA

RED SEA

1

A Glimmer Down Below

Discovering a cache of Roman coins and a new life

Caesarea Maritima as it is now. The remains of the
amphitheater are top center. PHOTO: RON BEN YITZCHAK

Heading back to shore, exhausted from an afternoon of snorkeling off
the coast, I see a flicker below. Diving down eight meters to investigate,
I grab a handful of sand near the light. After surfacing, I stare at my palm.
There in front of me is a gold coin with a head in relief. On its edge are the
Latin letters "IMP.CAES." I can't believe my eyes. I was snorkeling in an
area that had been the harbor of the Roman city of Caesarea two millennia
ago. Was this inscription short for "Imperial Caesar" and could I possibly
be looking at a gold Roman coin?

I found that coin in August 1968, when I was a twenty-one-year-old
Californian studying archaeology in Tel Aviv University's overseas student

program. I was camping in Caesarea with friends, including my future wife, Sharon. A half-hour drive south of Haifa, the city had served as the Roman capital of ancient Judea. In the present day it is a prospective World Heritage antiquities site.

I still remember the rush I felt as I opened my palm that afternoon a half-century ago. I mustered all my strength to make another few dives and by the end of the day I had what appeared to be five gold Roman coins in the pocket of my cut-off jeans. I had the presence of mind to get my bearings using prominent shore markers so that I could find the spot again.

Thus began an odyssey that changed my life forever, leading to a career exploring nature's underwater treasures and introducing thousands of others — including statesmen and celebrities — to the world of the deep.

My find left me with a swirl of questions: Did I have to report the coins? Would I be allowed to keep them? If so, what would I do with them?

The next day, I visited the Tel Aviv home of a friend's father, who collected ancient coins. I drew the coins from a leather pouch in his dining room and placed them on the table. He gasped as they glimmered in the lamplight. After peering at them through a loupe, he identified them as gold Roman *aurei* (coins), minted between the 1st century BCE and the beginning of the fourth century CE. Moreover, he assured me the coins were mine since I had found them at sea and not dug them up on government property. A decade later, Israel enacted a law to make such finds the state's property.

At the collector's suggestion, I showed the coins to Dr. Arie Kindler, the curator of the Kadman Numismatic Museum in Tel Aviv. Kindler was also excited by the number of coins I had found, their fine condition and apparent age. I agreed to loan them to him for a week to study and photograph. In January 1969, Kindler's article about the find was included in a quarterly publication of the Israeli Numismatic Society, leaving my name out at my request. I later donated a gold coin to the museum in appreciation for its help.

I could not wait to return to Caesarea and resume the search. I was a struggling overseas student with a tiny stipend for my basic needs and a university scholarship covering a dorm room shared with two others. But it was not the prospect of riches that drove my treasure hunt. Instead, it was the thrill of recovering exquisite relics that had lain on the seabed for thousands of years!

Gold Roman coin from the time of Emperor Trajan (98–117 CE).

I hitchhiked with Sharon to the ancient Roman site. Once in the water, I spotted familiar contours on the seafloor, but this time, I had no flicker of light to guide me. I eventually found another dozen coins. Exhausted, I returned to the beach with the treasure stuffed in my pockets as before.

Sprawled out on the warm golden sand, catching my breath after hours of diving, I wondered how the coins had ended up here. Had they tumbled out of the disintegrating wreck of an ancient ship that had lost its way in the fog and crashed against the nearby rocky reef? The site was just a few hundred meters from the harbor built by Herod the Great, ruler of ancient Judea (modern-day Israel) at the time of Jesus. Or had rising sea levels flooded a cache of coins hidden by a Roman nobleman during an attack on the city?

Lessons from Hadji Baba

Our hair still wet from diving, Sharon and I took a series of buses to the Old City of Jerusalem, with its many Arab antiquity dealers. We were excited and nervous. I stashed the coins in my jeans pockets, fearing someone would steal them. It was the longest two-hour ride of our lives. We entered the Old City — captured by Israel the year before — through the Damascus Gate and stopped at the first promising shop.

The sign read "Hadji Baba, Jerusalem Antiquities." The narrow shop was packed with beautiful ancient glass, shimmering gold and silver, bronze, antique jewelry, clay pottery vessels and ancient coins. Hadji Baba, a short but imposing man, greeted us graciously although I imagined him thinking, "What could these two hippies possibly want from me?" He offered us tea, as was the custom, and then we got down to business. I pulled a coin from my pocket and placed it on his ornate desk. To this day, I can still picture his eyes widening and beads of sweat forming on his ample forehead.

Even as experienced a trader as he was, his expressions and manner were a dead giveaway. He was impressed. Dodging his many questions about where I got the coin, I simply said I found it in the sea. I did not disclose that I had another sixteen in my pockets. After two cups of tea, I sprung the question that had brought me into his shop, "What is the coin worth?" Seconds ticked by as he contemplated his answer, keeping me in suspense, and explained the many factors that affect a coin's value: its rarity, condition, date of issue and weight; how long the emperor it depicted had ruled; the most recent sales price of a comparable coin. He said mine had come from the two-decade reign of Emperor Trajan (98–117 CE). Then, he finally pronounced, "This coin could fetch a price between $500 and $1,000."

My heart raced at the estimate, but I tried to appear calm and indifferent — as if I could conceal that I was little more than a naive college student. I had left California for the yearlong overseas study program with just $500 to my name. Hadji told me that coins stuffed in my pocket were worth $8,500 to $17,000. Sensing my emotions, Sharon squeezed my hand to settle me down. Hadji wanted to purchase the coin on the spot, but I told him I wasn't ready to sell. I assured him that his shop would be my first stop when the time came. We said goodbye. My bladder and heart were bursting. At least I could relieve my bladder at a nearby restaurant, but my heart was still in overdrive. We visited several other antiquity dealers and the same ritual followed. By the end of the day, I had a reasonably good idea that the coins were worth at least the price Hadji had suggested.

I continued freediving in Caesarea for more coins. Even though I was in decent shape, I could only spend limited time underwater. Still, the coins piled up in a safe deposit box I rented in Tel Aviv. When I needed cash, I sold them to Hadji and other dealers and collectors for $500 to $1,000 each. Later, I learned some were worth a lot more. But I was happy to have my own Roman "ATM" just a dive away in the waters off the coast of Caesarea.

With Sharon outside the antiquities shop of Hadji Baba in
the Arab market in the Old City, Jerusalem, in 1968.

Part of the horde of Roman coins I found dating back two millennia.

My sales trips to Jerusalem were exotic, scary and bizarre. Hadji Baba remained my primary buyer. His shop was along the Via Dolorosa in the shadow of one of the Stations of the Cross, an appropriate setting for selling coins minted during the period Jesus had taken his last steps. Hadji's was not the tiny enterprise it appeared to be. A hidden door opened to a labyrinth of passages lined with storerooms that few were allowed to enter. Once we began trading earnestly, Hadji would escort me to an office deep inside, where I would unveil my latest finds. Magnifying glass in hand, Hadji would examine every detail of each coin and rattle off the names of the Roman emperors they depicted — Caesar Augustus, Tiberius, Claudius, Nero, Galba, Otho, Vitellius, Vespasian, Titus, Domitian, Nerva and finally Trajan. He spoke of them with familiarity, as if talking about contemporary Middle East leaders.

Sharon often accompanied me on my sales rounds, but then a close call left me fearing for her safety. I was on the verge of concluding a transaction with a dealer when I learned I could get a much better price elsewhere. I felt free to pull out, as I had not signed a contract or made the obligatory hand-shake. The dealer felt otherwise and sent some employees to track Sharon and me down. Seeing them following us, we fled down the narrow stone streets and eluded our pursuers by ducking into a small restaurant. Once inside, we sought out a table in the back, out of view from the street, and sat with our backs to the entrance. We buried our heads in the menu and prayed the pursuers would not enter and harm us. It was the most nerve-wracking plate of hummus we ever ate.

Impressing the British Museum

Having sold a few more coins during the winter break to pay for a European trip, I took along a few coins to have them appraised outside of Israel. In Rome, I visited Trajan's column, built in honor of the Roman emperor whose image appeared on the very coins I had in my pocket. A friend took a photo of me holding one up as I stood next to his statue.

After Rome, I flew to London and visited the British Museum, home of one of the world's largest collections of ancient Roman coins. I wanted to meet the curator. But looking like a character out of the musical *Hair*, which had just opened in a West End theater, I was not exactly welcomed. Only after I showed the receptionist some of my coins did she agree to set up a meeting. The curator was fascinated by my story and asked if he could borrow a coin for further examination. He confirmed its authenticity the next day and referred me to several coin publications and auction reports. From them, I could see what I had suspected — the Jerusalem dealers had been offering prices twenty to twenty-five percent below world market value.

Once back in Israel, I continued diving through the spring and summer of 1969, adding to my trove of coins. I then returned to the States to complete my anthropology degree at California State University, Northridge. I left most of my coins locked up in the Tel Aviv safe deposit box, ready for my planned return after graduating the following summer.

In the meantime, I prepared to explore the treasure site in Caesarea properly by enrolling in a scuba diving certification course at the Beverly Hills YMCA. Little did I know then that diving would become my life's passion and livelihood.

A Roman coin featuring Trajan's column on the reverse, and
holding a Trajan gold coin at Trajan's statue in Rome.

Snorkeler.

2

Diving Through the Millennia

Now trained in scuba, I extend my explorations

Diving with Sharon.

With a university degree and scuba certificate in hand, I returned to Israel in June 1970. My baggage included two scuba tanks and two complete sets of dive gear. Brimming with confidence, I started teaching diving just months after getting my basic diving license in California. I gave my first lessons at a local pool in Israel. My first two students were Sharon, who was soon to be my wife — and lifelong diving partner — and Alex Shell, the pool's lifeguard, who would become my first assistant instructor and a lifelong friend.

Not long after, I returned to Caesarea. Diving with scuba gear was a different experience. Freediving had left me exhausted after just an hour, with the constant finning and breath-holding between the surface and seafloor. Now, instead of having to go up for air every minute or two, I could remain submerged for an hour or longer and thoroughly work the site. Sharon sometimes accompanied me. Scuba diving is done in pairs for safety and other reasons. Sharon and I, of course, were more than buddies. My passion for diving could easily have doomed a relationship. But sharing this mind-boggling adventure enhanced ours.

When diving conditions were good, we would spend hours underwater, using my two diving tanks and sometimes borrowing others from friends. Whenever I turned over a stone or pile of sand, fish would swarm in the hope of something to nibble at. They were harmless. Less so, though, were the spiny sea urchins that pricked my fingers as I searched the rocky crevices. Some days were excellent, such as when I found a pocket of ten to fifteen coins in a crevice. On others, I combed the bottom for hours, finding the debris of several millennia instead of coins.

Fortunately, we hit it off both below and above water.

Crusaders to commandos

You would not know from its tranquil appearance Caesarea's stormy past. King Herod the Great built the city and named it for his patron, Emperor Caesar Augustus, about the time of Jesus. At its height, it was the capital and main port of the Roman province of Judea and a center for early Christianity. A millennium later — after repeated destructive invasions — crusaders rebuilt it, only for the city to be razed in the 1200s by a Mamluk Muslim army. In the late 19th century, Bosnian Muslims established a small village on the crusader-era ruins. In 1948, Israeli commando forces led by Yitzhak Rabin, the future prime minister, captured it in the War of Independence.

I found artifacts ranging from pottery shards and a die made of lead (possibly from an ancient gambling den) to more recent relics such as ships' riggings and a boat ladder, which I used as a location marker. I was surprised to find two gold Byzantine coins, which are much thinner and less impressive than their Roman predecessors. Since the coins were from eras six hundred years apart, I speculated that they might have belonged to a Byzantine collector who had buried them for security. Where I was diving might have been dry land two millennia ago.

LEFT: Gold Roman *aureus*: Caesar Augustus (27 BCE–14 CE).
RIGHT: Gold Byzantine *semissis*: Constans II (641–668 CE).

I turned up gold coins from the reigns of nearly two dozen emperors, from Caesar Augustus (27 BCE–14 CE) to Trajan (98–117 CE). Four reigned in 69 CE alone, a tumultuous year of rebellions, palace revolts and assassinations. I found coins depicting all four of them.

Dayan's dealer

Tipped off by a collector, I turned to a new dealer, a courtly, silver-haired gentleman named Yoav Sassoon. An Israeli Jew of Iraqi heritage, Sassoon had been trading in antiquities for twice as long as I had been alive. He did business out of his home in West Jerusalem — where I felt much safer walking around with gold coins and thousands of dollars in cash than I had leaving Hadji's shop in the Old City.

Sassoon's apartment was as exotic as his building was nondescript. The spacious flat had the feel of a museum, with its displays of ancient clay, glass, bronze and copper relics — and of his specialty, gold, silver and bronze coins.

Our meetings would start with a familiar Middle East ritual: Sassoon, wearing a caftan or silk pajamas, would engage me in small talk over coffee or tea. He told me about his famous customers, including the legendary General Moshe Dayan, then the Israeli defense minister, and Dayan's latest antiquity exploits. Then, we got down to business.

"Let's see what you have here," Sassoon would say. I would then open my James Bond-style Samsonite briefcase and remove a velvet pouch containing the coins (by then, I had graduated from stuffing them in my jeans pockets). Using his loupe, he would inspect each coin and explain its significance and that of the emperor in relief upon it. For me, each transaction was an education.

During one session, we were interrupted by a phone call after reaching a deal on several coins. After Sassoon hung up, he apologized and escorted me to the door. As I was leaving the building, a big American car pulled up. A familiar figure wearing a patch over his left eye stepped out and hurried up the stairs. It was General Dayan, evidently pursuing another acquisition.

It was quite an experience for a 23-year-old kid from Los Angeles.

General Moshe Dayan, Israeli defense minister and avid antiquities collector.

ILLUSTRATION: SHLOMO COHEN

3

Call it Chutzpah!

With minimal training I launch Israel's second diving school

Mediterranean Diving Center at Sidna Ali Beach, Herzliya, in 1971.

It came to me in a dream. Intending to become an Israeli citizen, I enrolled in a Hebrew language program with other young immigrants in the southern Israeli town of Arad. I was twenty-three years old, with an anthropology degree and no clue as to a career. But I had fallen in love with diving after repeated visits to my underwater treasure trove. One night in this desert town of all places, I dreamt of establishing a diving center and school in Israel. It was a crazy dream, but the more I thought about it, perhaps it wasn't so crazy after all.

At the time, Israel was home to only one diving school, located in the Red

Sea port city of Eilat. The next day, I packed my bags, told the institute's managers I was checking out, and headed for Eilat. After a few hours' drive, I was at the counter of Aqua Sport Eilat, chatting with Israel's pioneer dive operator, Willy Halpert.

Willy seemed quite amenable to my opening a branch of his diving school along the Mediterranean coast. Thinking back, I scratch my head in wonder at my chutzpah. Only half a year after obtaining my basic scuba certification in California, I was negotiating to open Israel's second diving school. I could barely speak a sentence in Hebrew. But my timing was perfect. Scuba was emerging as a popular sport in the United States and Europe. It was only a matter of time before the boom would hit Israel.

After a toast to our partnership, I drove five hours to our home in Herzliya. Sharon and I shared a small cottage in this mid-size town with a beautiful beach front, a twenty-five minute drive north of Tel Aviv. I surprised her with the announcement that we were going into business. While Willy promised to follow up quickly with a contract, the next few months brought excuses and delays. Organization was not Willy's strong suit. We would become good friends, but not partners. Still, I was more determined than ever to fulfill my vision.

Meanwhile, I continued diving for Roman treasure, setting aside the proceeds to fund my dream. One day, while I was filling my air cylinders in Tel Aviv, a casual chat turned that dream into reality. Yobi Efrat, another early pioneer of Israel's diving industry, owned a compressor repair business and one of the few places in Israel outside of Eilat where divers could fill their tanks. When I told Yobi about my plans, he instantly realized what my business would do for him. The next thing I knew, he ushered me into his car and sped through the streets of south Tel Aviv, our destination: Sheba Trading Ltd, one of only three firms at that time importing diving gear into Israel. Yobi introduced me to its owners, Natan Vardi and Yitzchak Kestenboim.

After several weeks of discussion, the pair agreed to back my initiative. Except for a compressor, which I purchased, they supplied all the necessary diving equipment for the school. They got a fifty percent stake in the business, and I got a percentage of the profit Sheba made selling equipment to my students. Out of this synergy — not that I knew the term at that time — the Mediterranean Diving Center was born.

Diving with my partners Natan Vardi and Yitzchak Kestenboim.

While organizing the business took just a few weeks, finding a place for it took months. I went from town to town along the Mediterranean coast, trying to persuade local officials to lease me a seashore site — the most valued land in Israel — for an activity they had never heard of. Had it not been for the intervention of a hero of the 1967 Six-Day War, who also happened to be an avid diver, I would still be chasing my tail.

Through my diving contacts, I met retired General Avraham Yoffi, a veteran diver and, at the time, director of the new Nature Reserves Authority. Yoffi arranged for me to meet with the mayor of Herzliya. The municipality agreed to lease a strip of land at Sidna Ali Beach, which lies beneath a mosque of that name built on a sandstone bluff. The property included a pair of prefab concrete structures perched on a rocky ridge just above the water line. I used one for my office, reception area and a small snack bar, and the other for the compressor and equipment storage. Also on site was a primitive bathroom and outdoor shower. Missing, though, were electric and telephone connections. We hooked up to a nearby phone line quickly, but we relied on a gasoline-powered compressor to fill tanks for the first few years.

At the end of 1970, we held a ceremony to open the diving center. The mayor cut the ribbon and made a long-winded speech to an invited audience, including notable people from the worlds of sport, media and Israel's tiny diving industry.

Now, we had to drum up business. I scoured the country for swimming pools where we could conduct diving lessons and recruit students. I spoke with universities, corporations and even kibbutzim. Within a year, our blue Fiat pickup truck made stops all over Israel for week-long or evening diving courses, culminating in open water dives in the Mediterranean opposite our center. We opened branches at Jaffa's ancient port and my favorite diving site, the Roman harbor of Caesarea. As we expanded, I hired veterans of Israel's version of Navy SEALs, the Shayetet 13 (13th Flotilla), as instructors.

Mediterranean Diving Center branch in Caesarea. Without electricity but with a phone line, I hung out my shingle and got down to work.

Instructing on the Sidna Ali beach just below our diving center.

At the time, Sharon was at university studying social work. We were married a few months after the diving school opened. Eventually, Sharon became Israel's first female diving instructor. Still, at this early stage, she spent weekends and all her free time with me at the diving center making sandwiches, helping fill the tanks, working the counter and doing whatever else she could to keep our young business afloat.

Initially, we concentrated our diving activities along Israel's Mediterranean shore, where the consumer base was. We were so successful that within a few years we no longer had the sea to ourselves, as competing diving centers and schools opened. But the biggest challenge was securing opportunities for our students to dive in open water, the final requirement for a license. The Mediterranean coast of Israel has few natural harbors or protected bays. In unsheltered areas, scuba schedules are at the mercy of sea conditions. Weather permitting, the Mediterranean offers some great diving, particularly for antiquities. Jaffa and Caesarea boast two of the world's earliest ports. But more recent history would lead to one of our most memorable adventures.

Preparing for a dive,
1960s-style.

4

First Forays into Sinai

Diving the Red Sea with a pair of grizzled warriors

The newly built road along the Sinai coast, cutting
through majestic granite mountains.

It has been over half a century, but my first dive at one of the world's top
sites still flashes through my mind. I had never encountered such magical
beauty. I was on a tour of Sinai with fellow overseas students in the spring
of 1969, less than two years after Israel captured the peninsula from Egypt.
At the southern tip is Ras Mohammed (head of Mohammed), a craggy cliff
towering over the Red Sea's cobalt blue and turquoise waters. Diving with only
a mask, fins and snorkel, I felt immersed in a giant aquarium filled with corals
and fish of every imaginable size, shape and color. Little could I imagine back

then that I would play a key role in making the remote southern Sinai and Ras Mohammed among the most desired destinations in the diving world.

Unlikely partners

Flash forward to the early 1970s when demand for diving sites sent me up and down the Mediterranean and Red Sea coasts seeking suitable spots. On some of these trips, my unlikely partners and mentors were two divers almost twice my age.

Micha Peri and Yitzchak Yaacov had been friends since their days as warriors in the Palmach, the elite fighting unit of the Haganah, Israel's pre-statehood defense force. Both were among the nation's most experienced divers and underwater photographers when we met.

Soon after our diving center opened, they came by to fill up their tanks. We clicked immediately and they invited me to join them on one of their diving sojourns to Sinai. That trip would be the first of many. We bonded over our shared passions for diving and nature photography, but otherwise, we were opposites. They were combat veterans my parents' age; I was a bearded veteran of protest marches, a free-spirited member of the Woodstock generation. I was just getting a business off the ground in a fledgling industry; Micha was among Israel's leading construction engineers; and Yatza, a nickname since early in his army days, was an active-duty brigadier general.

Those long road trips to the Sinai coast were heaven — not only for the spectacular scenery and the diving but also for the opportunity to hear the veterans' tales of growing up during the British Mandate and fighting for Israel's independence and security.

With its dramatic granite mountains and rugged ravines, Sinai was unlike any place else I had visited. Most memorable were scenes of the indigenous Bedouin tribesmen riding their camels through the desert and the remnants of the many wars fought over the territory. The wreckage of Egyptian tanks from the 1967 war sat astride our dive site at Marsa Bareika, a bay next to Ras Mohammed.

Ras Mohammed is a diver's paradise.

Sinai Bedouin atop their camels, like a scene out of *Lawrence of Arabia*.

Abandoned Egyptian tanks from the Six-Day War
next to our dive site at Marsa Bareika.

Diving pioneers Micha Peri, front, and Yitzchak (Yatza)
Yaacov, far right, gearing up for a dive.

Micha was among the Palmach commandos who had disguised themselves as the crew of the refugee ship *Exodus*, the inspiration for the Leon Uris best-selling novel of the same name and its movie version starring Paul Newman. In another dramatic episode, at the close of the War of Independence in March 1949, Micha participated in Israel's "Iwo Jima" moment. He was part of the Palmach unit that captured Eilat, which would become Israel's southernmost port and crucial connection to Asia and Africa. Micha shot the historic photograph of his comrades planting a makeshift Israeli flag on the shore of the Red Sea. The banner was fashioned out of a bedsheet and ink by several female Palmachniks and has since become known as the Ink Flag.

LEFT: Remnants from past wars. RIGHT: The Ink Flag made from a bedsheet after the 1949 capture of Eilat. PHOTO: MICHA PERI

Yatza, who fought in Jerusalem during the War of Independence, earned an engineering degree at Massachusetts Institute of Technology (MIT) and became the deputy chief scientist of the Israel Defense Forces. In the years after we met, he paved the way for Israel's high-tech revolution as Chief Scientist at the Ministry of Commerce and Trade. But whatever I learned of the men's exploits, I had to pry out of them. They were friendly, kind and modest. Self-assured, definitely, but self-effacing as well.

"Yatza's Cave"

Our expeditions began with Yatza pulling up at the diving center in Herzliya in his army-issue, olive-green Plymouth. We would pack the trunk with scuba gear, pick up Micha at his home in Tel Aviv, and make the eight-hour journey through the Negev desert, past the port of Eilat and into Sinai. Sometimes, with Yatza's devoted driver at the wheel, we would travel overnight to a promising location around Ras Mohammed, take two dives, and return that same day. I would sleep most of the way home with a big smile on my face.

Micha and Yatza showed me some of their favorite sites. One of the most spectacular was a cavern reaching deep into the coral walls northwest of Ras Mohammed. "Yatza's Cave," as we called it, abounded in multi-colored soft corals and translucent sweeper fish.

My "internship" with Micha and Yatza did much to help forge my future in diving exploration and services. They connected me to people at the highest levels of government and commerce. The Israelis have a slang term for networking, *protectzia*, meaning access to the right people to get things done.

Micha and Yatza continued to dive and cruise with me into the 1990s. I owe them much.

Yatza's Cave in Marsa Bareika, named after the diver who discovered it.

5

Finding the *Farouk*

Searching for sponges, we discover a wreck

MV Farouk, flagship of the Egyptian Navy.

In 1972, French entrepreneurs contracted my friend Moshe, an Israeli fisherman, and I to explore the waters off the Gaza Strip. While the assignment was to find sponge beds, we contributed the epilogue to the most significant naval exploit of Israel's War of Independence.

Leaving from the beach in Gaza City, Moshe and I took an inflatable craft to a fishing boat crewed by local Arabs. After an unsuccessful search for sponges in deeper waters, we headed for a site three kilometers from shore that one of the fishermen said teemed with fish. After diving in, Moshe and I were surprised by the sight of a shipwreck twenty-five meters below. The broken remains sat upright on the sandy bottom, tangled in fishing nets.

Wary of being snagged by the nets and concerned that my tank was half empty from the sponge search, I kept my dive short and returned later for a thorough exploration.

Launching our inflatable off Gaza beach.

A local fisherman hands Moshe his diving tank.

Looking back at the wreck during my ascent, I saw a tantalizing sight: an object resembling a deck gun eerily shrouded with fishing nets and lines. Could this have been a military vessel? As I researched possible wrecks off Gaza, I learned about the *Emir Farouk*, once the flagship of the Egyptian Navy. Subsequent dives confirmed that the wreck was, in fact, the *Farouk*.

LEFT: Deck gun on the *Farouk*. PHOTO: DAN ARAZI
RIGHT: Torpedo boat being lowered into the water. PHOTO: ISRAELI NAVY

LEFT: Explosive charge on a torpedo boat.
RIGHT: Commander Yochai Ben-Nun. PHOTOS: ISRAELI NAVY

In October 1948, the warship ferried five hundred men to reinforce Egyptian troops in Gaza. No match for the *Farouk*, which was accompanied by a minesweeper and another vessel, the small Israeli Navy resorted to unconventional tactics. Under cover of darkness, a mother ship lowered four explosive-laden motorboats to the sea. Each one was piloted by a single commando for the hour-long journey to the *Farouk*. When the first two commandos were within one hundred yards of the Egyptian target, they locked their steering wheels and jumped off. The boats made direct hits, sending the *Farouk* to the Mediterranean floor.

That was the last known sighting of the vessel until our dive in 1972, which happened to occur on the sixth anniversary of the Israeli capture of the Gaza Strip during the Six-Day War. The next time I returned to the site, I brought along a TV crew. Our efforts ignited exciting media coverage about Israel's first naval heroes and their daring feats.

A few years later, my then business partner Yossi Kivshany, a reserve officer with the Israeli version of Navy SEALS, the Shayetet 13, retrieved the ship's wheel, some helmets, galleyware and other equipment.

While the *Farouk* wreck was an exciting discovery, the waters off Gaza were not a viable destination for diving tourism — even back then. Someday, I hope we can return and dive there in peace.

The commando team with Israeli Prime Minister David Ben Gurion (center). PHOTO: ISRAELI NAVY

6

Making a Home in Sinai

Learning as we go, we bring diving tourism to the Red Sea

Poster promoting Eilat featuring my photo.

When it came to diving activity in Israel in the early 1970s, all eyes and fins pointed to Eilat, Israel's port city on the Red Sea, a five-hour drive or less than an hour's flight from Tel Aviv or Jerusalem. The water was calm and clear year-round, and the coral reefs were abundant with tropical fish.

As we were on the verge of setting up a branch of the Mediterranean Diving Center in Eilat, Israeli government officials suggested another site: the new Sinai settlement and tourist village of Neviot, located a fifty-minute drive south in the Nuweiba Oasis. Eager as we were to establish a foothold along the Red Sea, we jumped at the offer.

Nuweiba sits on an alluvial flood plain, wedged between stark granite mountains and the aquamarine waters of the Gulf of Aqaba. Across the narrow gulf lies Saudi Arabia, easily visible to the naked eye. The plain was formed from the sediment deposited over the millennia by flash floods overflowing the part-time canyon riverbeds known as wadis.

Two Bedouin fishing villages, Nuweiba Tarabin and Nuweiba Muzaina, lie to the north and south of Neviot, respectively, nestled into a desert oasis reaching the water's edge and shaded by beautiful date palms. The Bedouin are masters of the desert with an uncanny ability to make the most of their inhospitable environs. They built their dwellings out of such materials as boulders from the floodplain, corals and shells from the sea, driftwood and palm wood. Although they can be fierce fighters, the Bedouin have managed to accommodate the region's shifting powers, be they Ottoman Turks, Egyptians or Israelis. The Israelis operated by a live-and-left-live policy during their fifteen-year rule over Sinai (1967–1982), encountering few, if any, political or security problems with the Bedouin.

The Israeli civilian administration provided the Bedouin with medical services and established schools in the larger villages. The burgeoning tourist industry provided jobs when, previously, the tribes had few sources of employment beyond the oil fields in the Gulf of Suez.

Run by idealistic Israelis in their twenties, Neviot originally served as a camp for the crews that built the coastal road from Eilat to Sharm El Sheikh in the aftermath of the Six-Day War. The young settlers took over the spartan wooden huts with ambitious plans of opening a *moshav*, or collective settlement, to raise crops and host tourists.

The tourist village offered us a small shack on the beach, a stone's throw from the coral reefs. In the spring of 1972, we opened the first Red Sea branch of the Mediterranean Diving Center. We began working through the backlog of students awaiting open-water training and certification.

The first group arrived during Passover, filling the village with students and their families. It became common to see our guests dodging camels as they made their way, scuba tanks strapped to their backs, from the diving center to the shallow waters off the beach.

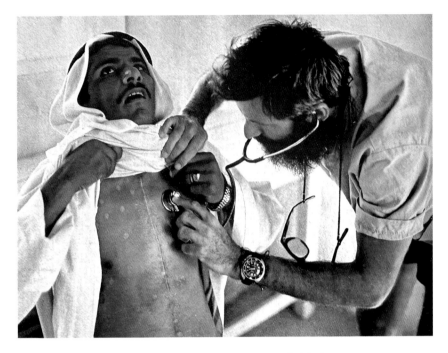

Israeli Dr Amnon Zvielli making a field trip to
Bedouin tribes. PHOTO: DAVID DOUBILET

Nuweiba on the Sinai coast. PHOTO: DAVID DOUBILET

Neviot holiday village in the early 1970s.

LEFT: Equipment in our Neviot diving base.

RIGHT: Camels became useful members of our team.

Realizing Sinai's enormous potential for diving tourism, we began promoting the Red Sea base to both the general diving public and alumni of our diving school. The shallow reefs were well-suited for snorkeling and scuba lessons. We could offer complete holiday packages with accommodation in the adjoining tourist village.

Over the following months, we explored all along the Sinai coast from Eilat in the north to its southern most point and Ras Mohammed.

In the fall of 1972, we booked our first group of American divers. To our surprise and chagrin, they arrived wearing steel helmets. In retrospect, I can understand why. In the wake of the Six-Day War, the Egyptians, on occasion, would shell Sinai, though not as far east as our dive site. By 1972, there was an uneasy peace, the calm before the next storm. Another war was the least of our worries. We had to prove to our American guests — and ourselves — that the diving was worth the effort and expense, not to mention that we knew what we were doing.

We traveled the 225-kilometer coastal road from Eilat to Sharm with boats perched atop our vans. The trip was punctuated by mishaps that could have doomed our fledgling operation, but all was forgiven thanks to the spectacular dives off the southern coast of Sinai.

The leader of the American group was Ken Seybold, a prime mover in the emerging diving tourism industry. Ken was not shy about offering suggestions for bringing our operations up to international service and safety standards. I appreciated his input; we were definitely on a learning curve.

Our army surplus outboard engine once conked out a mile offshore. Crew members jumped in the water and paddled furiously with their fins toward the beach. Luckily, the one speedboat within fifty kilometers came to our rescue and towed us in.

No one from the tour group was with us for the scariest moment of the trip. As I took our van around a dangerous turn while descending a steep mountain road, the boat tied to the roof slipped its ropes, slid forward and blocked the windshield. I managed to bring the van to a stop on safe ground. The boat was dinged a bit, but we could make it seaworthy without inconveniencing our guests.

We host our first group of American divers, seen here diving at Coral Island.

The Americans' leader Ken Seybold rides a camel.

Ras Mohammed — the very site where only three years before I had made my first Red Sea dive — was the culmination of a ten-day safari. There at Shark Reef, the beach leads into the shallows of the coral shelf. Farther out, the water shifts from aquamarine to cobalt blue, where the reef suddenly plunges hundreds of meters into the abyss. With a visibility of up to fifty meters, divers are treated to a dazzling array of colors. Multi-hued hard and soft corals cover the vertical wall, competing for attention with exotic tropical reef fish and large schools of territorial and pelagic fish, including barracudas, tunas and sharks.

Undaunted by our mistakes, Ken encouraged us to move our diving operations to Sharm. He told me that the trip convinced him that the southern Sinai around Sharm and Ras Mohammed offered the best diving in the world, and he wanted to book tours with us starting the following season.

Heeding his advice, I moved our Red Sea operations to Na'ama Bay, Sharm El Sheikh, in early 1973. After that, we never looked back.

Ras Mohammed at the southern tip of Sinai.

Shore diving for the hearty, near Nuweiba.

7

The Boxcar on the Beach

Turning Sharm from battleground to playground

Heading out for a dive from our boxcar diving center.

Before Israel captured Sinai in the Six-Day War, Sharm El Sheikh (Bay of the Sheikh) consisted of a seasonal camp for nomadic Bedouin tribes, a UN naval base and an earthen airstrip for small planes.

In the early 1970s, Israeli military personnel stationed at the army, air force and naval bases accounted for most people living in and around Sharm, as most people call it. The southern tip of Sinai was a key strategic location where war was an ever-present threat.

With no movement toward a peace treaty with Egypt, Israel had constructed a road connecting its Red Sea port city of Eilat to Sharm El Sheikh. The asphalt strip would enable the southern Sinai to be turned from an historic battleground into an international playground. No place better symbolized the transformation than the Straits of Tiran, where Egypt had triggered wars in 1956 and 1967 by blockading Israeli shipping. Tourists now snapped photos of divers wading into the Red Sea just below decommissioned cannons.

The Sharm area became home to several hundred civilians, mainly government officials, construction workers, merchants and employees of the military bases. When we arrived in 1973, Israelis were setting up Ofira, a town named after the biblical port of Ophir, which in 1000 BCE was the farthest destination of King Solomon's Red Sea trading fleet (the exact location is a matter of debate).

As the ultimate fate of Sinai was yet to be decided, no one was willing to invest in permanent structures for tourism. Many of the accommodation buildings were designed to be portable, ready to be trucked to Israel proper should Egypt regain sovereignty.

Pre-1967: A small UN base sits on the isthmus
(narrow strip of land) between the bays of
Sharm El Sheikh and Sharm El Moya.

Short commute: Our trailer home was steps from the diving center.

Tourists inspect an Egyptian cannon overlooking the Straits of Tiran.

Life on the frontier

"Downtown" Ofira boasted the Moses Hotel, a rough-and-tumble collection of wooden rooms crafted out of materials from an abandoned road construction site. It would have been lucky to rate a half-star.

Then there was the aptly named Caravan Motel in nearby Na'ama Bay, which consisted of thirty small trailers still sitting on their wheels. A large inflatable hanger-like structure served as its dining room, staffed by local Bedouin dressed in traditional flowing white gowns known as jellabiyas and head coverings called keffiyehs.

Next door was the equally "elegant" Marina Sharm Hotel. That consisted of thirty ugly prefabricated multicolored fiberglass geodesic domes.

Fortunately, aesthetics was not our primary concern; making a viable business was. We obtained permission to set up shop in a dilapidated storeroom behind the Marina Sharm. We changed our name from the Mediterranean Diving Center to the more apt Red Sea Diving Adventures. We handed over our previous diving center to the Nuweiba holiday village. With Na'ama Bay as our new home base, we had world-class diving at our doorstep.

Initially, we made do with the stuffy storeroom, and I slept in my Fiat 238 double cabin van. After a few months, the hotel manager informed me that he had obtained a more permanent diving facility. It turned out to be a wooden World War I-era railway freight car. It was delivered by a huge semi-trailer and unceremoniously dumped on the beach meters from the water's edge.

Overcome with excitement and naivety, I savored the moment. Here I was, at the ripe old age of twenty-six, in business and right in the heart of perhaps the best diving destination in the world.

The converted train car, about thirteen meters in length, accommodated our compressor, tanks, scuba gear and rental equipment for snorkelers. For the first year, beach sand was our floor. I persuaded local construction crews to bring me excess cement, which I dumped into the sand daily until we had a proper floor. We also had a small workshop for repairs and a tiny kitchen that we added to the train car for preparing meals for our staff. We "borrowed" electricity for the compressor by running a high-voltage electric line under the beach sand to the hotel's generators, one hundred meters away.

One of my customers offered me a tiny travel trailer — my "villa on wheels" — which I parked next to the train car and turned into my living quarters. The commute to work would not be a problem! The trailer was the size of a VW van; it had room enough for all the amenities I needed at the time, except a phone line, running water and air conditioning. Sharon eventually joined me, somehow squeezing in. We lived in the trailer until our first child Ayelet was born in the spring of 1974, when we moved to a government-owned apartment.

For ground transport, we bought an army surplus jeep. We painted it orange so it would be visible to an aerial search party if we ever got stuck in some god-forsaken desert wadi. Our version of the American Automobile Association (AAA) motor club was a Bedouin camel capable of pulling the jeep out of the sand.

We purchased a few homemade boats, locally known as "hasakas," which could hold up to ten divers and their gear. Four meters long by two meters wide, they were basically giant surfboards — with gunnels just a few inches above the water line — powered by outboard motors. Later, we added other small craft and eventually fancier vessels between ten and fifteen meters in length outfitted with a cabin, small galley, a head (toilet) and shaded deck space. Luxury.

Our army surplus jeep and local towing service.

Rebuffing the Navy

Even with our earliest boats we could explore reefs that up to that point had been difficult, if not impossible, to reach by jeep — a tantalizing attraction for our clients. But the Israeli Navy had other plans and sent a directive confining our diving activities to Na'ama Bay. Furious, I thought this restriction would kill our business. After consulting with our staff, I decided to run the naval "blockade."

The morning after the Navy's dictate, we traveled to one of the closer dive sites just outside the bay. A patrol boat spotted us and pulled alongside. By loudspeaker, its skipper ordered us to return to the bay. I shouted back that the Israeli government wanted to attract tourists to Sharm and that they wouldn't come if they were confined to the bay. Unmoved by my patriotic appeal, the skipper insisted that we obey his orders. Startling our onboard guests, I told him he would have to arrest us first.

Clearly upset, the skipper radioed his base in Sharm for instructions. His commander said he would deal with the matter later and instructed that we be left alone. That night, I was summoned to the Navy base, where I met with the commander, his senior staff and Sinai's civilian administration representatives. I bluffed my way through a spiel about how I was showing influential guests the area's potential for diving tourism. I said that if they were impressed with the sights — and the cooperation of local authorities — Sharm could look forward to thousands of visitors.

After consulting with their high command, the Navy dropped its objections. We were now free to dive wherever we wanted along the Sinai shore. It was a victory for us and for the others who would follow in our wake.

Dive instructor Zvika Lahav (left) and myself (center)
head toward one of the early "surfboard" boats.

The area around Sharm with local dive sites.

Skippering a flat boat out to a reef.

8

War Comes to Sinai

From diving to driving during the Yom Kippur war

Our trusty blue van was converted from a diver carrier to an ammo carrier.

At about six-thirty on the morning of Yom Kippur in October 1973, an Israeli Defence Force (IDF) officer knocked on the door of our home in Herzliya. Sharon answered — I was still fast asleep after making the eight-hour drive from Sharm the day before. The officer announced that Egyptian forces were massing along the Suez Canal and war was imminent. He presented a draft notice, not for me but for my vehicle, a Fiat 238 double cabin pickup truck.

Just ten days before, during Rosh Hashanah (Jewish New Year), Sharm was crowded with tourists, most of them Israelis. With the one hotel and one motel at capacity, hundreds of families camped out in tents along the area's beaches.

Among the visitors was the IDF chief of staff, Lt. General David (Dado) Elazar, who was having a great time water skiing next to our diving center. If Dado had any clue of an impending war, he did not show it. Indeed, I had hoped to have the honor of taking him diving, but that did not work out. In the calm after the New Year's rush, I decided to drive home and surprise Sharon. I arrived just before sunset, the beginning of Yom Kippur.

So there I was the following day, staring at the draft notice for my pickup. Putting my deflated ego aside, I realized that as a new immigrant, I had yet to do my basic army training — so, as far as the IDF was concerned, I did not exist. On the other hand, my pickup very much did; it was subject to conscription for the transport of munitions, supplies and even soldiers.

I insisted my beloved pickup wasn't going anywhere without me as the driver. The Israeli army was legendary for turning conscripted civilian vehicles into useless wrecks during wartime. I grabbed my favorite pillow (first things first), packed a small suitcase of clothes and went off to my first war, volunteering to drive my commandeered pickup.

I spent the first night sleeping in the Fiat at a base in the south near Sinai. The following day, it was loaded with munitions — a jarring sight, considering the big orange words emblazoned on the side of the truck: Mediterranean Diving Center.

The base officers put up with me for a few days and then advised me that my services were no longer needed. I kissed my wheels goodbye and hitched my way back home. The Fiat survived the war in reasonably good shape and I even received compensation for its use.

After getting "fired" from my brief stint as a supply driver, I sought a way to support the war effort. I came up with the idea of entertaining troops with stories of my underwater experiences and showing them slides of the marine life of the Red Sea. After all, that was what I knew best. Through friends, I learned that the army designated units of the entertainment corps to appear before soldiers with post traumatic stress disorder. After making my pitch, I was invited for an "audition," drafted on the spot and presented a schedule for reporting to rest and recreation centers.

For the remainder of the war, Sharon and I made nightly presentations all over the country, driving with blacked-out headlights on roads crammed with tank transports and military convoys. We gave a one-hour slide show at each stop titled "Fantasy Under the Sea."

Some of the soldiers were in wheelchairs or swathed in bandages; others were coping with invisible but equally devastating wounds from the trauma of war. My slide show featured calming images of tropical fish and colorful corals; I also slipped in a few topless mermaids. The latter got their attention. Soldiers will be soldiers, regardless of their wounds.

In southern Sinai at the outset of the war, Egyptian jets were shot down in dogfights and the IDF repelled air-dropped commando units. One Egyptian MIG was downed a few hundred meters offshore from Ras Mohammed. The intense combat lasted just a few days and Sharm suffered minor damage.

LEFT: The tail section of an Egyptian MIG shot down over Ofira. PHOTO: IDF SPOKESPERSON'S UNIT. RIGHT: The primary military communications system in the center of Ofira was strafed on the first day of the war.

I rushed back to Sharm after the area was reopened to civilians. Fearing the worst for the diving center, I was surprised to find it mostly unscathed. On the morning the war broke out, my loyal Bedouin worker, Juma, scoured the bay for any rental gear we had out. He tossed all the equipment into the train car, locked the big heavy doors, dropped the keys off at the hotel reception desk, and high-tailed it to his parents' village in the Sinai mountains. We had a joyous and emotional reunion when he stopped by the diving center several months after the war.

While peace returned to Sharm, it was many months before the tourists did.

Anne with the
Doubilets' camera gear.

9

Exploring with *National Geographic*

Our center is put on the world diving map

Ras Mohammed. PHOTO: DAVID DOUBILET

As a child, I did my diving vicariously through Jacques Cousteau's books and documentaries, the adventures of Mike Nelson as played by Lloyd Bridges in *Sea Hunt*, and the pages of *National Geographic*. It was a dream come true when I became part of those pages.

In the summer of 1974, a team from the iconic magazine arrived at our base in Sharm, marking the start of a collaboration that would put Red Sea Divers — as we were now often referred to — on the map and alter the course of my professional career. The team consisted of Dr. Eugenie (Genie) Clark, a renowned scientist and author of the bestselling books *Lady with a Spear* and *Lady and the Sharks*, and photographer David Doubilet, assisted by his wife, Anne.

I had met the trio the previous year at the annual Sea Rovers diving show in Boston. A strange set of circumstances ushered me, then an unknown diving entrepreneur from the Red Sea, onto the speaker's platform. Sharon and I were staying with friends in Boston. Our host, an employee of the Israeli consulate, knew someone at *The Boston Globe* and arranged for me to be interviewed. An excellent half-page article appeared a few days later.

By chance, the event's organizer was Jewish and wanted to promote anything associated with Israel. He sought me out and invited me to give a slideshow at the conference, among the first, if not the first, presentation in the United States about Red Sea diving tourism.

That year, the conference's guest of honor was Dr. Genie Clark, and the featured speaker was my childhood hero, Jacques Cousteau. My spot on the bill was right after Cousteau — a tough act to follow! After my presentation, Genie approached me with the Doubilets in tow. Genie was diving into unexplored waters off Egypt's Red Sea coast when I was a toddler. David and Anne were both about my age and already successful underwater photographers. At twenty-seven, David had his first cover image for *National Geographic*, accompanying a story by Genie on the sleeping sharks of the Yucatan, Mexico.

Now, these veterans of the deep were telling me about plans for a *National Geographic* story about diving in the Red Sea. When they asked me if I would provide support and guide the expedition, it took me about three seconds to say, "Yes!" We initially set a date for late 1973, but then the Yom Kippur War intervened.

The following summer, the team finally drove up to Red Sea Divers, equipped with a dozen cases of the finest underwater photo equipment. It was worth more than the entire diving center. My crew had never seen anything like it before. Conversely, our dive base must have come as a shock to our well-traveled visitors. We had been operating in the Red Sea for barely two years, and out of Sharm for only one. The diving center was still housed in the fifty-year-old railroad freight car, and our meager gear amounted to little more than twenty dive tanks, a small compressor and a boat that resembled an oversized surfboard.

Equally unimpressive was our land transport, a temperamental, beat-up army surplus jeep. For accommodation, the trio had but one option: the ill-suited fiberglass geodesic bungalows at the Marina Sharm Hotel next door. Fortunately, Genie, David and Anne were great sports and consummate professionals. They were focused on their mission: diving, research and photography.

The Shark Lady

Just a few inches over five feet tall, Genie was so dedicated to her work that you never wanted to disappoint her. Known worldwide as the Shark Lady, she was beloved by all who knew her well. She had a great smile and loved to laugh and play practical jokes. As her accent betrayed, Genie grew up in a working-class neighborhood of New York City. Still, she was comfortable courting the super-rich and famous to advance both her research and environmental protections. With the help of philanthropists Anne and William Vanderbilt, Genie founded what is now known as Mote Marine Laboratory in Sarasota, Florida.

Genie's research countered the demonization of the shark as the merciless eating machine epitomized in *Jaws*, the blockbuster movie released in 1975, the same year *National Geographic* published the first of many Red Sea articles we would collaborate on.

Over three months, Genie, the Doubilets and I dived up to four times a day. Every evening, we would plan the dives for the following day. Our principal sites were Ras Mohammed, located at the southernmost tip of Sinai; and the Straits of Tiran, comprising four coral islands in the middle of an international shipping channel between Tiran island and the Sinai shore. Two other favorites were Ras Um Sid, with its steep wall of giant Gorgonian fan corals, and the Temple, both sites lying a short boat or jeep ride from our diving center in Na'ama Bay.

Lady with a Spear — the book that made Genie Clark
famous. Genie beaming. PHOTO: DAVID DOUBILET

The mating game

We spent much time exploring the steep coral walls at Ras Mohammed, where one of our most memorable dives was at Shark Reef. Known for its massive walls plunging vertically from the surface to a depth of over one hundred meters, it is among the most stunning reefs in the diving world. Easily accessed from the shore, it is covered with dozens of species of soft and hard corals of every possible tropical color: shades of red, orange, yellow, green, purple and white. Clownfish, butterflyfish, angelfish, groupers, gobies, blennies, stingrays, wrasses and giant moray eels abound. They, in turn, attract pelagic hunters like tuna, jackfish, barracuda and sharks.

I led the team, with Genie at my side and the Doubilets just behind us. Descending the wall on one occasion, Genie grabbed my elbow with one hand and pointed down with the other. Just below us, two dozen gray reef sharks were swarming in a frenzy, some seeming to attack one another.

I signaled to Genie that we should immediately dive down to get a closer look, but she restrained me. She motioned our group to nestle in the crevices of the nearby reef wall. Soon, the sharks moved in our direction, continuing their strange behavior as David snapped photo after photo. We were so excited by the spectacle that we sucked our diving tanks dry and had to rely on snorkels to make the long swim back to shore.

Afterward, Genie was beside herself with excitement. What we had just witnessed, she told us, was shark foreplay. What I mistook for attacks were actually "love bites" — males putting moves on prospective mates. Genie said she had seen such behavior in lemon sharks in pens at her research center, but to her knowledge, this was the first time it had been witnessed in the wild. She said that had I approached the sharks I might have scared them away and spoiled our chance to capture their performance on film.

Reef shark with "love bites."

Diving the Temple.

Temple worshippers

Another favorite destination was the Temple, named for several large adjoining coral mounts. The formation rises to just below the surface in eighteen meters of sheltered aquamarine water. It attracts congregants representing the full range of Red Sea tropical fish. Often, at the end of an intense day of diving the deep waters off Ras Um Sid we would decompress at this site, enjoying its tranquility and beauty while blowing off the nitrogen buildup in our bodies.

In the bright desert sunlight, the vibrant colors of the Temple overwhelmed the senses. Fish darted in and out of the coral cover, seeking food and safety. The larger pelagic hunters cruised along the reef wall alone or in schools on their endless quest for a meal. Below ten meters, the red and orange colors started to fade; at thirty meters, with dwindling sunlight and the aquamarine water, almost everything would take on a blue-green hue.

Diving at night revealed a very different world. In the dark, marine life and tropical colors are visible only within the beam of a powerful flashlight. Depending on the diver, night diving can feel exhilarating or claustrophobic. At Temple, nocturnal hunters like sharks, eels and octopus prowled the waters as lobsters and crabs poked along surfaces. Parrotfish retreated into crevices or caves, secreting a mucous-like envelope or "sleeping bag." Light attracted the small, nearly transparent glassy sweeper fish and shiny silversides. They, in turn, drew lionfish, which swept in for a meal right before our eyes.

As an added treat, the Red Sea had its own light show: marine life emitting bioluminescence and fluorescence, especially under the ultraviolet beams that we would sometimes take with us. These created a stunning display, lighting up the corals with a whole new color palette of green, red, orange and yellow. Sometimes during a full moon we would turn off our torches and be guided by the moonlight through the crystal clear waters, following each other's outlines as we disturbed the bioluminescent plankton. An eerie and memorable experience.

South Sinai diving sites visited by the *National Geographic* team.

Straits of Tiran and Saudi Arabia's Tiran and
Sinifir islands. PHOTO: DAVID DOUBILET

Enlisting the Navy

With *National Geographic* as our client, we were able to persuade the Israeli Navy to transport us to more distant dive sites like the Tiran Straits and Tiran island, at the time beyond the reach of our small boats. On one trip, I managed to sweet-talk a patrol boat commander to sneak about a kilometer into Saudi waters to the reefs off Sinafir island. While it may seem we were tempting fate, the Israeli Navy ruled that remote part of the Red Sea, and the Saudis rarely ventured there.

We made two dives into the shallow waters surrounding the reefs, which appeared untouched by human hands and fins. The corals teemed with tropical reef fish, barracuda and reef sharks. There was even a dugong, a rare marine mammal that is a cousin to the Florida manatee and a distant relative of the elephant. The dugong is very docile and easy to approach, more interested in grazing the sea grass beds than curious divers swimming nearby. That is why many countries have enacted laws to protect these peaceful animals. Regulations prohibit touching, firing a camera flash at them or even approaching too closely.

Dugong in the shallows grazing on the sea floor.

"Raptures of the deep"

As experienced divers, we knew how to make the most of our air supply. We would stay submerged on shallower dives for up to two hours on a single tank, more than double the average bottom time. Occasionally, we would dive in excess of sixty meters, much deeper than recreational limits.

Before one dive into a deep canyon at Thomas Reef in the Straits of Tiran, Genie asked me for a favor. Professor Charles M. Breder Jr., the retired director of the New York City Aquarium and the man Genie credited as her most influential mentor, would soon be turning seventy. She had prepared a waterproof birthday card that she wanted me to photograph her holding at seventy meters. I agreed, but reluctantly.

Divers using compressed air risk intense nitrogen narcosis at such depths, a syndrome commonly known as "raptures of the deep" because of its intoxicating but perilous symptoms. There are anecdotes about delirious divers trying to share their air with fish using their regulator mouthpieces.

Genie and I found a sandy patch between the coral heads to take the picture. As I was setting up the shot, I noticed that she was staring at me with a dazed expression instead of unfurling the card. Fearing the worst, I rushed over and took her by the elbow. I then began a controlled ascent, closely watching Genie's eyes and breathing. By the time we had reached thirty-five meters, she gave me the diver's OK sign. Enormously relieved, I jotted a question on my waterproof slate, asking if she still wanted a picture with the card. She smiled and motioned yes. She sent her mentor the photograph and the card, with its inscription implying it had been taken seventy meters underwater. The actual depth remained our little secret.

***

One of my most important duties for the *Geographic* team was chief schlepper, responsible for getting David and Anne's elaborate underwater photo gear to the right spot at the right time. I was well rewarded. David triggered my passion for underwater photography and gave me my first underwater camera, a Nikonos II. Anne taught me about macro photography, the art of extreme close-ups. After finishing the assignment, David unstrapped his Rolex Submariner diving watch and handed it to me. It has been on my wrist every day since, experiencing more than 10,000 dives in nearly half a century. Definitely the nicest gift I have ever received.

"Strange World of the Red Sea Reefs" was the cover story of the September 1975 issue of *National Geographic*. Genie wrote in the text accompanying a gallery of photos by Anne and David: "If I could dive only one spot in the world, I would choose Ras Mohammed."

I was thrilled to be identified in the article as the diving pro who cared for the team and to appear as David's main diving model (the photo is *on page 75*). He and the article's writer, Dr. Eugenie Clark, autographed a copy for me. Needless to say, I was also delighted by the attention the article drew to the Red Sea Divers Center.

NATIONAL GEOGRAPHIC

Date	Title	Authors
Nov. 1974	The Red Sea's Sharkproof Fish	Dr. Eugenie Clark/David Doubilet
Sept. 1975	Strange World of the Red Sea Reefs (Cover)	Dr. Eugenie Clark/David Doubilet
Nov. 1978	The Flashlight Fish of the Red Sea	Dr. Eugenie Clark/David Doubilet
Aug. 1981	Sharks: Magnificent and Misunderstood	Dr. Eugenie Clark/David Doubilet
Apr. 1982	Eternal Sinai	David Doubilet
July 1983	Life in an Undersea Desert	Dr. Eugenie Clark/David Doubilet
Nov. 1993	The Red Sea (Cover)	David Doubilet
Mar. 1995	Journey to Aldabra	David Doubilet

Articles in *National Geographic*.

Voyager — the ride of a lifetime!

From the deep … to deep space. The 1974 *National Geographic* expedition to Sharm catapulted me fifteen billion miles from Earth, give or take a few million miles. Not me literally, but my photo. Unbeknown to me, David successfully entered a competition to include an image in the time capsule placed on NASA's *Voyager 1* space probe. The capsule, which takes the form of a twelve-inch gold-plated copper disk, contains pictures and sounds representing the life and culture of Earth. Launched in 1977, *Voyager* was the world's first interstellar space vehicle.

David's image immortalizes me at the entrance of an underwater cave surrounded by glassy sweeper fish. It can be found along with other pictures from the time capsule in the book *Murmurs of Earth: The Voyager Interstellar Record* by the astronomer Carl Sagan. If you want to check out where *Voyager* — and my photo — is now, visit voyager.jpl.nasa.gov

The image by David Doubilet chosen both for the *Voyager* time capsule and September 1975 *National Geographic* article.

Two decades with the dream team

Over the next two decades, Genie, the Doubilets and I continued to work on articles for *National Geographic*. We spotlighted the Red Sea Moses sole, which secretes a milky substance that can repel a shark just as its jaws open for the kill. At the suggestion of famed Red Sea naturalist David Fridman, we profiled a creature that glows in the dark, aptly called the flashlight fish.

Genie holding a flashlight fish. PHOTO: DAVID DOUBILET.

Genie jots notes in the background as students help with her research.

The four of us also teamed up on nature conservation projects, such as helping to end illegal shark fishing in the Red Sea. Sharks are prized for their meat, skin and teeth. When our Red Sea Divers crew noticed fishermen setting long shark lines next to our diving sites, I enlisted the *National Geographic* team to document the abuse. Setting out one morning with cameras ready, we found sharks thrashing about in gruesome agony, trying to free themselves from the big hooks that meant certain death. We sent the images to the nature authorities and persuaded Bob Simon, then CBS bureau chief for Israel, to report on our efforts to save the sharks. The publicity blitz worked and the shark fishing operation was shut down.

David (right) photographs Genie holding onto a reef shark
snagged on an illegal fishing line. Anne is in the background.

In the April 1982 issue, *National Geographic* covered Israel's withdrawal from Sinai. The story included pictures of my young family snorkeling and of the Red Sea Divers Center at Na'ama Bay.

Working with *National Geographic* was exciting and educational for myself and my crew. We provided essential services and received lessons from masters in marine biology and underwater photography. It was a symbiotic relationship — just like so many others in the sea.

With the *National Geographic* team in 1977 aboard a Red Sea Divers boat
(from left): David Doubilet, Genie Clark, me and Anne Doubilet. Hillel is driving
the boat. Sitting in front is my dad, Murray Rosenstein, who was visiting.

In tribute to Genie Clark: with me in 1974. PHOTO: DAVID DOUBILET;
and in 2014, the year before she died at ninety-two. PHOTO: OLGA TORREY

10

Nudes in the Red Sea

How I became a professional photographer

Shooting nudes in the Red Sea for *Oui* magazine.

So I was out in the Red Sea with beautiful Israeli women wearing only their smiles. They were models for an underwater shoot for *Oui* magazine, a *Playboy* subsidiary, and their photographer had panicked moments into his first dive. What was I to do?

I should start at the beginning. In 1974, one of our instructors, Shimon Dotan, received a call from Marvin Newman, who had shot the "Girls of Israel" for *Playboy* (April 1970). Now, the famed American photographer wanted to do another nude shoot in Israel, underwater in the Red Sea. Fine with us.

We were contracted to supply diving support services, equipment and boats to access the sites for the shoot. Marvin, his production team and several gorgeous Israeli models descended on our diving center. Their visit did not create the stir one might expect. By then, in Sharm, it was not unusual to see beautiful women sunbathing in the nude. The next morning, we headed out for the first day of shooting.

Operating one of the dive boats, I brought along my diving gear and the Nikonos camera I had just received from the *National Geographic* photoshoot in the hope that Marvin would allow me to shoot him shooting the girls. The idea was for Marvin, assisted by Shimon, to photograph them from every conceivable angle as they frolicked among colorful corals and tropical fish. Things turned out differently than planned. It transpired that Marvin had never scuba dived before. It is one thing to strap on a diving cylinder and go down a few meters with an instructor hand-in-hand, what we would call an "intro dive," but taking images underwater is an entirely different matter. And Marvin needed not just snaps but high-quality photographs for a famous magazine.

Within a minute underwater, Marvin's mask filled with water and he swallowed some seawater. Panicking, he shot up to the surface. Although I was still a novice underwater photographer, Marvin asked me to take over. I did not spend a lot of time bargaining over the fee.

Nikon designed the Nikonos camera for underwater photography. Since each roll of film had only thirty-six shots, I had to make several dives — and pray the exposures were correct. We stayed in relatively shallow water with excellent ambient light. Concentrating on the subject matter was not a problem.

Needless to say, it was a very unusual day of diving. I faithfully handed over all the slide rolls I had shot to Marvin, who packed and left with his models. I never did learn whether the images were deemed worthy of publication. But it was the first of many paying jobs I would have as an underwater photographer — and one of the most memorable.

11

Diving Mount Sinai

Enlisted to help fix a well, I am out of my depth

Saint Catherine's monastery at the foot of Mount Sinai.

In 1975, the Sinai Development Administration (Minhal, to use its Hebrew acronym) contacted me about finding a volunteer scuba diver to extract a damaged water pump from a well outside Saint Catherine's Monastery. Since the ranks of visiting divers were still small at that time, I offered my own services. Besides, how often does one have a chance to dive at the foot of Mount Sinai? And for our daughter, Ayelet, what a spot to celebrate her first birthday, beneath one of the holiest sites in the world, where the Bible says Moses received the Ten Commandments.

The Minhal sent a Bedouin driver to our diving center to pick us up. It was no easy trip back then — even for a Dodge Power Wagon with four-wheel drive. Much of the route was off-road, along twisting, boulder-strewn wadis punctuated by several harrowing ascents and descents. But tumbling off a

Sinai cliff was the least of my worries.

Throughout the bumpy six-hour drive, my mind was churning with worries about something a Swiss guest at the diving center had told me when he heard about our trip. He cautioned me to make sure I would dive according to high-altitude decompression tables. I had never heard of this before and asked if he happened to have those tables with him. He smiled and answered, "What for? I came here to dive the Red Sea; no need for such a thing." For those six hours we spent bouncing through Sinai, I was freaking out at the thought of diving into an ancient well, fifteen hundred meters above sea level, without knowing if I'd wind up with a bad case of the bends.

We arrived just before nightfall and were put up in a clean but spartan room next to the local ranger station. We lit one candle on the crumbling cake that Sharon had baked for the occasion. That night, exhausted from the long drive but excited and anxious about what the next day would bring, I could hardly sleep. When we awoke, we were dazzled by the sight of the monastery's ancient granite and sandstone walls turned gold by the dawn light. The early spring air was crisp and cool, and the deep blue sky was almost entirely cloud free.

After checking my gear, I hopped into a civilian administration jeep to drive to the well. The pump had been damaged the week before when flood waters swept debris down the shaft. A maintenance worker briefed me on the lines and pipes I would need to cut to free the pump. He gave me a hacksaw to supplement my dive knife. After putting a harness over my wetsuit I was lowered by rope to the water level, fifteen meters down. Diving several meters below that, I reached a wooden platform. To squeeze past it, I had to remove my twin tanks and push them ahead of me. Then, after remounting the tanks, I descended another ten meters through the crystal clear, chilly water to the pump. Now, the real fun began.

The pump was attached to more pipes and lines than I was told in the pre-dive briefing. Unsure they all needed to be cut, I had to resurface, again removing and replacing my tanks to wiggle past the platform. Reaching the water's surface, I shouted my questions through the echoey shaft. Embarrassed and apologetic, the crew explained what I needed to do. But my problems weren't over.

Getting ready to
head down.

Instead of the clear artesian water of my first descent, the water was murky from the silt I had stirred up on my first trip. It was like being blindfolded. I would have to do everything by memory and feel. Shaking off fears that I was about to end my Red Sea diving career at the bottom of a Bedouin well, I began sawing through the pipes. When I turned to the cables, I muttered a prayer that someone above had turned off the power and sliced through them. After what seemed like an eternity, I freed the pump and connected it to a towing cable.

For the fourth time, I maneuvered myself and my equipment through the narrow gap by the platform and then ascended to the surface. I still had a few hair-raising moments as I was lifted out of the well by a rope attached to a jeep via a pulley. The cord held; I could relax for the first time in over an hour. As the support crew pulled up the pump after me, I felt both a sense of mission accomplished and one of chagrin that I had ever taken on the job in the first place.

Ill-trained and ill-prepared for this type of job, I had been way out of my depth. I had descended twenty-five meters to recover the broken pump. It's a good thing I got away with not using those decompression tables.

Before heading home, a monk gave us a tour of the fourteen-hundred-year-old monastery, including its famed library of ancient manuscripts and early printed books. On display in another room was a rather more macabre collection — the skulls of monks from centuries past.

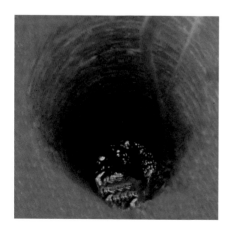 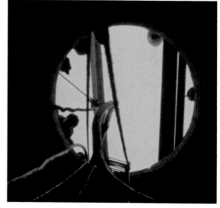

LEFT: The view down the well. RIGHT: The Bedouin looking down at me (photo taken from the waterline).

Success: Posing with the pump and my technical support team after the dive.

LEFT: Being lowered down by the Bedouin. **RIGHT:** Skull room in the monastery.

My scary thought was I may have ended up there if I had drowned in the well!

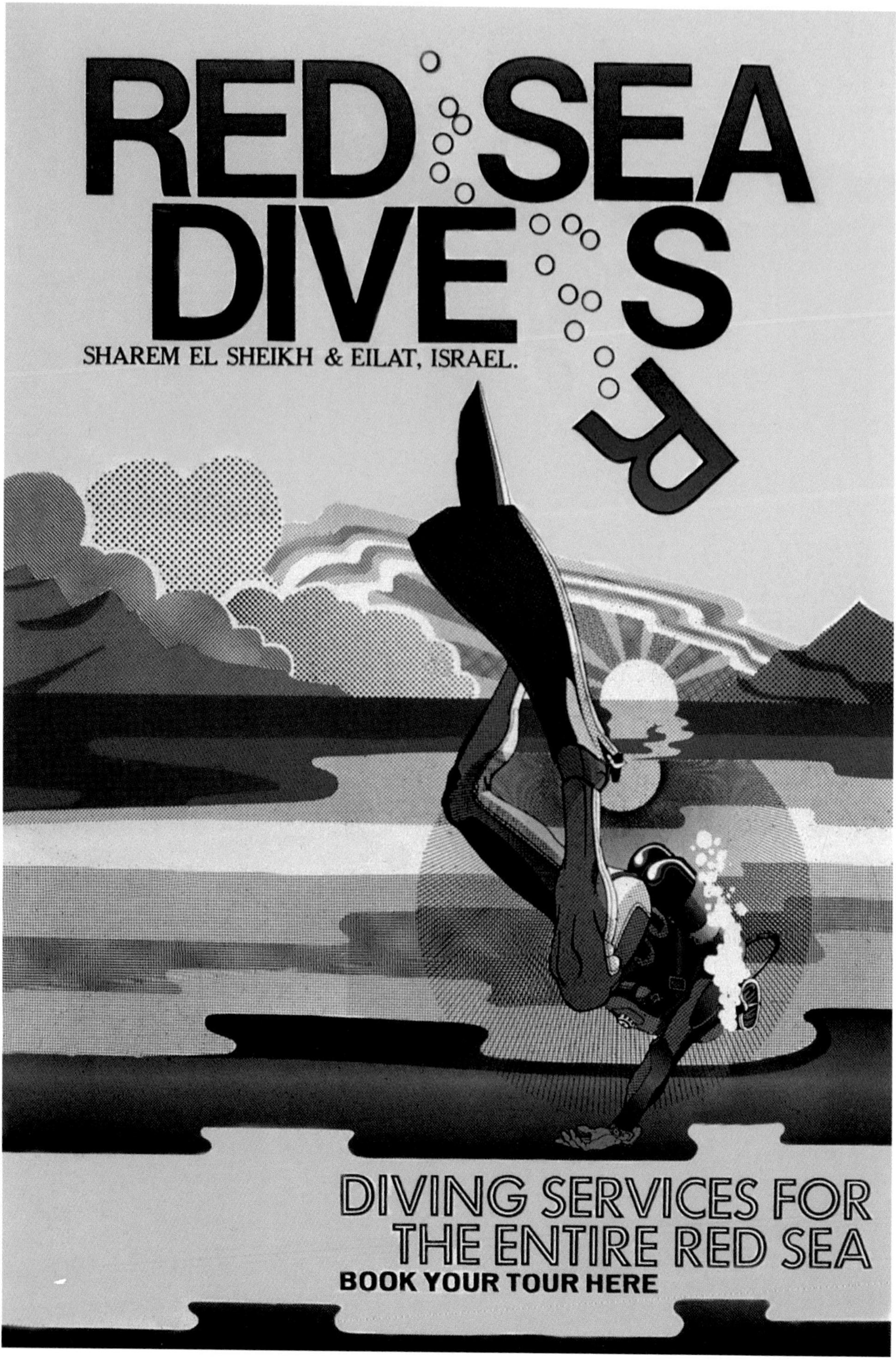
RED SEA
DIVERS
SHAREM EL SHEIKH & EILAT, ISRAEL.
DIVING SERVICES FOR
THE ENTIRE RED SEA
BOOK YOUR TOUR HERE

12

Our Dream Base

Revamped Red Sea Divers welcomes the world

The new Red Sea Divers Center on the left, the Marina Sharm
Hotel with its geodesic dome bungalows to the right, and our
dive boats on the beach for periodic maintenance.

I often wondered what was on the minds of our guests after they had traveled thousands of miles to our fledgling dive center in Sharm in the early 1970s, only to see an ancient wooden boxcar and the tiny trailer Sharon, baby Ayelet and I called home. It was quaint, if you were of a positive mindset, but primitive. Our resources were limited and business was hard to come by, especially after the 1973 war with Egypt when months went by without a foreign diving tourist. Still, we hung in there and slowly but surely the business rebounded and grew.

Then came the cover feature on Red Sea diving in the September 1975 *National Geographic*, which put us in the spotlight of the international diving community. That year, I brought in two partners: one contributed money, the other hands-on experience. The working partner, Yossi Kivshany, was a former officer in the Israeli Shayetet 13, i.e. Navy SEALS. A master diver, Yossi took on running our nationwide network of diving schools based out of a new office in Tel Aviv and the original center on the Mediterranean at Herzliya's Sidna Ali beach.

With the cash injection from the other partner, Michael Daniel, we built a spacious diving center with a restaurant and bar in front of where the boxcar had stood. Our guests from the early days must have been in shock when they saw the latest incarnation of the center completed in 1976 and officially renamed Red Sea Divers.

Our own united nations

The new center consisted of six prefabricated rectangular buildings arranged in a U-shape. The open part of the U featured a courtyard and garden overlooking the turquoise waters of Na'ama Bay, a mere forty meters away. To give the concrete prefabs a more local and natural feel, we collected driftwood from Tiran island to decorate the walls and make furniture for the patio restaurant and bar.

When we first opened, the crew consisted of Sharon and me, assisted by Chmeed, a local Bedouin. By the mid-1970s, we had ten to fifteen full and part-time employees to house and feed.

A full-time cook managed the restaurant, often a local housewife or someone from Israel proper. Sharon would fill in when staffing was short. The menu was basic: turkey schnitzel, hamburgers, hot dogs, pasta, rice, soups, salads and plenty of fish and chips. The restaurant also made lunch boxes for the divers' day trips.

Our international crew included backpackers who worked a few months at a time, former Israeli SEALs, veteran skippers and even former clients. I sensed that many were motivated not by the pay but by the once-in-a-lifetime work experience in a diving paradise, or simply wanted to escape the chilly winter months in Europe.

We employed local Bedouin, sometimes three generations of men from the same family. They were an inseparable part of the Red Sea Divers family. We learned much from them about the desert and how to make the most of limited means, especially in the early years. By working at the dive club, they picked up skills, languages and other talents that would serve them well in a more modern and swiftly changing Sinai. They affectionately called me Abu Dhegan (the bearded one) — a moniker I took on with pride.

Many memorable personalities worked for us over the years — perhaps no one more so than Natan Zahavi, who managed our restaurant/bar and later became one of Israel's most famous radio personalities. Natan would let off steam by slinging a kitchen knife at the door next to my office. One day, as I opened it, I barely evaded a dagger headed straight for my head. It missed my nose by centimeters before spearing the door.

At times we served as hosts and surrogate parents, social workers and disciplinarians — occasionally having to break up fights between our intoxicated guests.

The dive center looking out across the patio.

Staff photo L-R: Sharon, myself, Rachel, Yossi, Ayelet, Agadi and Chmeed. Dive guide Liz Cooke filling tanks with our new compressor.

No experience needed

The shallows in the bay in front of our diving center were perfect for diving courses. As students advanced, they dived along a reef just off our beach. We gave diving theory lessons — necessary for certification — in an air-conditioned classroom or on our large, shaded patio. Once we were up and running, we trained and certified hundreds of divers a year.

For certified divers, we offered a complete selection of rental equipment, including two hundred shiny new aluminum diving cylinders. We purchased the most powerful air compressor in the Middle East, capable of filling a scuba tank in less than a minute. For non-divers, we offered windsurfing, water skiing and glass bottom boat excursions.

Fits and starts

We not only expanded our base but also our range. With our sights on more distant dive sites, we invested in our land and boat fleet to transport our clients safely and comfortably. Just as we had a pair of new GMC vans with trailers on order, the limits of our existing transport nearly cost us a lucrative customer.

We had been diving mainly from sites adjacent to the shore, relying on jeeps with trailers and Dodge Power Wagons. On one outing, we escorted a leading European dive travel operator as he checked out the prospects for bringing groups to dive with us in Sharm. Naturally, we wanted to show him Ras Mohammed. It was an hour-and-a-half jeep ride, half of it over desert tracks that skirted Egyptian minefields laid down before the 1956 and 1967 wars. Just a kilometer from our destination, our army-surplus vehicle overheated and stopped.

His face turning red under the powerful sun, our European guest must have been wondering how we would get out of this fix. Sensing a potentially lucrative contract slipping through my fingers, I suggested we walk the remaining kilometer to the dive site while our Bedouin driver sorted out the problem with the motor. The travel operator, sweat beading on his forehead, looked at the diving equipment and then at me. He shrugged as if to say I was crazy to think we could lug all that gear to the site. Fortunately, our crew included two instructors, Nir Avni and Zvi Agadi, still in shape from their days in the armed forces. I pointed to them and told the agent that all would be fine. So off we went, taking an ample water supply just in case.

Just as we reached the shoreline fifteen minutes later, I heard music to my ears: the sound of our jeep catching up with us. By the day's end, Ras Mohammed had worked its charm. The operator was beside himself with what he had witnessed during his two dives there. By the time we made the uneventful drive back to the club, the day's transit problems were a distant memory; over pre-dinner drinks, our guest announced that the following year, he planned to send at least two groups a month to dive with us. I assured him reliable vehicles were on the way and there would be no more surprise stops in the middle of nowhere.

Long-distance diving

Besides the new land transportation, we bought larger, more seaworthy vessels. The first was a forty-foot (twelve-meter) wooden fishing boat built in Cyprus that most recently had worked the waters off Israel's Mediterranean coast. We trucked it down to Eilat, where the boat underwent a total refit to prepare it for its new purpose, diving tourism.

Any vessel not designed for diving had to be modified. We maximized the deck space, adding benches for seating and awnings to protect against the brutal summer sun. We installed storage space for gear; staging tables for preparing cameras and other equipment; a secure ladder and platform for diving; rinse tanks for gear; a first aid kit; and a ship-to-shore communications system.

After stocking the boat with supplies and spare parts, we cruised to our base in Sharm. Reflecting our aspirations to expand the fleet, we changed its name from *Etti* to *Red Sea Diver 1*.

We now could cruise south for an hour and a half to Ras Mohammed or head north for an hour to the Jackson, Gordon, Thomas and Woodhouse coral reefs in the Straits of Tiran and the rarely visited reefs of Tiran island itself.

Red Sea Diver 1, our first proper dive boat, alongside
a dinghy for ferrying guests and gear.

Part of the Red Sea Divers fleet (from left): glass bottom
boat, *Red Sea Diver 1* and *Red Sea Diver 2*.

Leased charter boats also worked for our operation. Loading
the boats using our jeep to move heavy cylinders.

Invoking Sinai Rule 950

Initially, we had to moor the larger boats in deep water because Na'ama Bay had no dock or jetty. We ferried divers and equipment out by dinghy, wasting time that would be better spent exploring the coral reefs. The civilian administration brushed off our appeals for help in improving tourist access.

In many respects Sinai was like the Wild West; sometimes, out of necessity, we had to take the law into our own hands. Such was the case when we set out to build a floating dock for our boats. We enlisted friends and colleagues in the construction business, enticing them with diving courses, boat excursions for their families and meals at our patio restaurant. The makeshift crew brought heavy machinery to construct a packed dirt road down to the water's edge, shored up by boulders from inland. It ended at a floating dock assembled from wooden beams and sealed flotation devices scrounged from construction sites.

We then braced for the response of the local authorities. Sure enough, a convoy of jeeps pulled up to Red Sea Divers the next day. Instead of parking in our lot, the jeeps drove up the new access road to the illegally built dock.

There, the officials held an impromptu meeting, which we viewed from the safety of our restaurant patio. After fifteen minutes, they drove back to the club, marched inside and congratulated us — with a wink and a smile — on a job well done.

Breathing a sigh of relief, I told them we were meeting the needs of our diving clientele and following Sinai Rule 950. Reuven Aloni, head of the Sinai administration, asked me what that rule was. I pointed to a Caterpillar 950 tractor parked nearby and pronounced, "In the Sinai, that is Rule 950!"

With pride, we placed ads in all the major diving publications to promote our expanded services and itineraries. That and my overseas appearances at dive exhibitions began to pay off. Our clientele soon included the period's top American dive tour operators — Carl Roessler of See & Sea Travel; Amos Nachoum of La Mer; Bob Goddess of Tropical Ventures; and Art Travers of Poseidon Ventures. One agency, HUB, specializing in travel seminars for diving doctors, brought over one hundred guests, our largest group ever. Upon their departure, our medical supplies quadrupled thanks to all the sample first aid kits and medicines left behind.

Loading a dive boat on our new homemade jetty.

A bolt out of the blue

In 1977, when I turned thirty, my dream of a world-class diving operation in the Red Sea was coming true. Red Sea Divers was serving hundreds of divers a month, not just from Israel but also from Europe, America and Asia — a truly international operation. We had a fleet of three dive boats of our own and three foreign-flag boats on charter; plus vans and jeeps for land-based trips.

But then came a bolt out of the blue: Egyptian President Anwar Sadat announced he was going to Jerusalem to address the Knesset. We welcomed the possibility of peace between the Middle East's two greatest adversaries, but we wondered what it would mean for Red Sea Divers. In the meantime there were many more challenges and adventures awaiting us.

IN 1943 J.Y.COUSTEAU INVENTED THE AQUA LUNG IN 1976 IT BECAME WORTHWHILE★

IN 1976 A PIONEERING GROUP OF RED SEA DIVERS CROSSED THE TIRAN STRAITS FOR THE FIRST TIME TO EXPLORE A CORAL PARADISE UNTOUCHED BY MAN. THE SUBMERGED CORAL ISLANDS EMBRACING THIS ANCIENT MARITIME PASSAGE WAS TO BECOME OVERNIGHT, THE MOST TALKED ABOUT AND REQUESTED DIVE SITE IN THE GREATEST OF MARINE PARADISES, THE RED SEA.

WARM WATER A tropical sea in the midst of a dry desert guarantees personal comfort both on shore and along the 200 miles of continuous fringing coral reefs, where water temperature is between 70°–80°F. throughout the year.

A QUIET SEA Diving off the Sinai is a diver's dream with little wave action and almost no current. Natures own built-in weather insurance-of 320 bright sunny days and cloudless skies guarantees 350 diving days a year.

FANTASTIC VISIBILITY Although experienced Divers have heard it all before, they're still startled to see our dive boats' anchor resting at 200 ft. while adjusting their masks at the surface.

TEEMING WITH LIFE 1000 species of fish have already been identified. divers are still discovering, photographing and naming new ones.

FOR SKIN DIVERS Fringing reefs provide accessible and breathtaking seascapes for snorklers. Glass bottom boats, sailing, windsurfing and water-skiing are also available.

HOTEL ACCOMODATIONS Although your diving sites are next to some of the most barren, intriguing and breathtaking mountain landscapes in the world, visitors find comfortable air-conditioned hotels and restaurants from Eilat to Sharem el Sheikh.

DIRECT FLIGHTS DAILY With EL AL Israel Airlines departing from N.Y. and in the immediate future from L.A. and Miami to the dreamland of the Red Sea.

RED SEA DIVERS GUIDE The producers of this pioneering guidebook in diving tourism spent 3 years in research and field surveys to describe, chart, illustrate, and photograph the diving sites of this area.

RED SEA DIVERS We are pioneers in Red Sea Diving and are the largest diving organization in the area. For the past 10 years we have been offering the finest in diving services to guests from all over the world. We operate 2 fully equipped Diving Centers: Red Sea Divers — Eilat, at the Gateway to the Red Sea and Red Sea Divers — Sharem el Sheikh, in the heart of the finest diving country to be found anywhere in the world.

Specializing in daily boat trips to one of over 50 unforgettable diving sites, Red Sea Divers treats the visiting diver with experienced and friendly guides, 250 sets of the finest American made diving equipment.

We have special programs for all interested Divers and groups. For complete information about our Boat diving adventures, Sinai safaris and famous "Red Sea Divers Guide" please send us the attached post card. Along with the answers to all your questions we will send you a small token from your friends in the Red Sea.

Contact our American representative: **Mr. Oren Most** 9200 Sunset Blvd. PH-9 Los Angeles, Calif. Tel (213) 9300137 Cable Seatelex, or **Red Sea Divers** El Al Bldg. Ben Yehuda St. 32, Tel Aviv, suite 506, Tel. 295529, 291858, Telex 32470 COIN I.L. AT. DIVERS.

For complete details and reservations contact our U.S. representative:
Red Sea Divers
9200 Sunset Blvd., PH-9
Los Angeles, Ca. 90069
Telephone 213-930137
Cable : Seatelex

Name_____Phone_____
Address_____
City_____
State_____Zip_____

RED:SEA DIVE:S

THE DREAMS YOU ARE DIVING ⟳ WE DIVE EVERY DAY EVERY NIGHT...

★ Quotes from some of our guests who spent time diving with us this past year.
CARL ROESSLER, author u/w photographer: "The diving couldn't have been more spectacular".
DR. EUGENIE CLARKE, ichthyologist, author: "If I could dive in only one spot in the world, I would choose Ras Muhammed".
DAVID DOUBILET, u/w photographer: "The reefs of Sharem combine the best elements of the finest reefs found the world over".
JACK MCKENNEY, film maker, past editor SDM: "If I had to choose one place to spend the rest of my diving days it would be the Tiran Straits".
DR. HANS HAAS, author, explorer, marine scientist: "The glimmering vision that rose up to meet me from the depths took my breath away.

SKIN DIVER FEBRUARY 1979 **41**

The full-page advert we ran in diving magazines.

13

Disaster Strikes

Our dive boat becomes a dive site

Red Sea Diver 2 shortly before it sank.

One morning, we discovered that the pride of our fleet, the newly
purchased *Red Sea Diver 2*, had vanished. My first thought was that
pirates had entered the bay overnight and absconded with the boat. But then
we spotted the top of a rope ladder floating next to the boat's marker buoy.
Diving into the water, I was shocked to see the *Red Sea Diver 2* five meters
below. Our dive boat was now a dive site!

In a panic, I called my partner Yossi Kivshany, a reserve navy officer, at
our Tel Aviv office. Yossi flew down the next day with Yohanan Spier, his
former commanding officer. After retiring from the Navy, Yohanan opened
a salvage company. We discussed various ways to raise the boat. But the
best method — sealing all the openings, pumping out water and pumping
in air — was unworkable in our isolated area. When Yohanan suggested

using flotation bags or oil drums to lift the boat, one of our divers, Elia Sides, came up with a solution: "borrow" a pair of shipping containers from a decoy Hawk missile battery not far from our dive center. The phony missile installation — the IDF's equivalent of a scarecrow (or scareplane) — was not secure and was often used by tourists for photo ops.

The challenge was finding a way to transport the canisters, which were five meters long and weighed one hundred kilograms each. By chance, our Bedouin watchman had an uncle who agreed to lend us his truck. We met at the diving center late that night and drove to the site. As it was not an actual missile battery, we did not have to worry about evading guards or climbing fences. We loaded up the first two canisters we came across, covered them with a tarp and headed back to the dive club.

At first light, we epoxied valves to the fiberglass canisters. After suiting up, we flooded the canisters and descended to the boat. We secured our makeshift boat lifts and pumped them with air to displace the seawater. Like magic, the boat rose to the surface. Once the deck was above the water line, we pumped the water from its bilges to refloat the vessel. We then used a tractor and discarded telephone poles to pull it to shore.

Then our problems began.

The military police happened to learn that a pair of Hawk missile canisters were lying on the beach just below our diving center. They asked us how the containers got there. I shrugged my shoulders but told the officers that we fully intended to file a complaint with the local authorities about military debris fouling our otherwise pristine beach. A truck was dispatched from a nearby army base and the beach was cleared that same day.

We repaired the engine and electrical systems within days and thoroughly cleaned the exterior and interior. Looking better than ever, the upgraded *Red Sea Diver 2* was back in action.

A diving tourist poses next to one of the decoy Hawk missiles. PHOTO: BRET GILLIAM

A Hawk missile canister attached to the sunken *Red Sea Diver 2*.

Red Sea Diver 2, after sinking and refit, especially the back
deck which was better for diving organization.

A school of glassy sweeper fish in a cave during filming of *Nomads of the Deep.*

14

The Red Sea on the Big Screen

Hollywood enlists our help

With pioneering underwater filmmaker Bruno Vailati.

It was to be my major motion picture debut. The year was 1976. Cue me, floating beneath the Red Sea with a dead fish between my teeth and a bunch more in a net bag attached to my weight belt.

Italian cinematographer and director Bruno Vailati — who made one of the first underwater feature films, *Blue Continent* (1951) — was touring the world's seas to film sharks, barracuda, polar bears and other notorious marine animals. He wanted to show how many of these creatures were not as menacing as the media made them out to be.

My star turn was to serve bait to a large moray eel lurking in its lair amid a coral reef. I was supposed to pull a fish out of my bag, wave it in front of an eel and stick it in my mouth. Bruno would film the moray coming at me as I chomped on the tail. It was a tricky shot with a significant time restriction, namely how long I could hold my breath. I had to remove my regulator to bite on the fish.

I located a moray tucked into a coral head. So far, so good. But just as the filming was to begin, I felt a strong tug on my bag of fish. Attracted by the scent, a white-tip reef shark snatched the bait bag from my weight belt and bolted, taking a free lunch at our expense. With no more fish, we had to quit for the day.

As it turned out, I appeared in only fifteen seconds of the film. I can be seen aboard our dive boat alerting Bruno — in impeccably dubbed Italian — to a shark's fin breaking the surface. I suspect most viewers were more interested in the blond diver in a scant bikini lying at our feet.

Feeding a moray eel while filming *Friendly Monsters of the Sea.*

Bruno Vailati filming *Friendly Monsters*.

Bruno's assistant, Swedish underwater cinematographer
Bengt Börjeson enticing an eel out of its lair with a fish.

The film debuted in 1977 as *Cari Mostri Del Mare* (Friendly Monsters of the Sea). You can catch a clip on my YouTube channel.

Tentacles

If you step into a seafood restaurant in Israel and see a life-size giant tuna made of fiberglass hanging as decoration, it may be a leftover prop from one of the worst movies ever. Trust me; I helped make it. *Tentacles*, released in 1977, boasted an all-star cast that included John Huston, Shelly Winters and Henry Fonda — and a preposterous plot. In this Italian-made *Jaws* knockoff, a mutated giant octopus rampages through a California seaside town.

A second unit crew filmed some of the underwater scenes in Sharm. Red Sea Divers provided diving and boat services. For us, it was a hilarious adventure that paid top dollar.

None of the stars made the long trek to Sharm, but their stunt doubles did. Nestore Ungaro, the underwater unit director, oversaw the production team, which included Italian divers who seemed more interested in having a good time than tackling the challenges of filming beneath the sea. Whenever they thought a task too difficult or dangerous, they would develop ear or tummy aches or some other inventive ailment.

The "pig" mini-submarine negotiates an array of tuna props.

Aside from tunas and the octopus, the Italians brought a "pig." This was a mini-sub developed and deployed by the Italian navy for commando operations in World War II. The sub got its nickname because it was so unwieldy underwater. In the film, the heroes manned the pig in a daredevil search for the octopus. I was disappointed that the Italians didn't leave us the sub.

While filming *Tentacles*, one of Israel's most famous actors, Uri Zohar, was vacationing in Sharm with his family. They stayed at the Marina Sharm Hotel, next door to Red Sea Divers. Early one morning, Uri entered our diving center just when the film crew was getting organized for that day's shooting. Surprisingly, some recognized him from movies screened in Italy and they invited him to hop aboard the boat and watch the making of *Tentacles*. He was delighted, entertaining everyone by speaking with a mock Italian accent. He didn't understand the language but spoke terrific gibberish, accompanied by all manner of Italian hand gestures.

Realizing that night was Christmas Eve, I radioed Sharon to see if we could host the homesick Italian crew for an impromptu party at our small Sharm apartment. Sharon, as ever the good sport, agreed. Uri got wind of the party and asked if he and his family could join us. The actor also brought along his mom and sang Christmas songs in his pseudo-Italian accent. I wore a Santa hat and covered my black beard with a fake white one. A punchbowl of grog got everyone in the holiday spirit. Our hospitality won us the affection of the Italians, who were much more cooperative for the remainder of the shoot.

It would be Uri's last Christmas party. Shortly after his visit, he began studying to become an ultra-Orthodox rabbi, shocking all of Israel.

Nomads of the Deep

Red Sea Divers helped make movie history in 1979 — and in the process, nearly grounded our boat and mangled a photographer. Chuck Nicklin, who had earlier been involved in a wreck discovery story that we will come to later in the book, returned with a Canadian team headed by filmmaker John Stoneman. They were making *Nomads of the Deep*, the first underwater film intended for the giant screens of IMAX theaters. The production chose two locations for the shoot: the ocean waters off the Hawaiian town of Lahaina, Maui, for its humpback whales; and Sharm El Sheikh, for its coral reefs and exotic marine life.

A huge waterproof housing was custom-made to immerse the 70mm IMAX camera. The entire apparatus, complete with lighting, was so heavy and bulky that we had to build a special crane for our forty-foot boat.

Besides the stunning Straits of Tiran and Ras Mohammed sites, we took the film crew to a secluded cave that we rarely showed to tourists. The area was exposed to the prevailing northerly wind, making it tricky to keep the boat in position. We could not anchor because of a one-hundred-meter sheer drop-off near the shore. After maneuvering the boat as close as possible to the cave, I signaled the team to jump in the water.

As our crew lowered the IMAX housing system, the boat drifted toward the reef. We came so close that I feared the vessel would crash into it and smash into smithereens. But with the camera crew still in the shallow water surrounding the boat, I worried that the propellers would slice someone if I revved up the engine. After the deck crew assured me no one was in danger, I pushed down on the throttle and missed striking the reef by barely a meter.

We hung off the steep coral wall at a safe distance until the camera crew started to surface. We had the filmmakers swim to us before extracting them from the sea. Once everyone and everything was on board, my heart rate returned to normal—until Flip Nicklin, Chuck's son, asked to speak with me in the wheelhouse. Flip told me he had been hanging just off the stern of the boat when he heard the motor put in gear. He hastily descended to avoid the propeller. Flip wasn't angry with me. Indeed, he was remarkably calm, but I was shaken up for days at the thought that I had come so close to maiming him or worse. Such was the drama behind the scenes of *Nomads of the Deep*, which went on to great success in IMAX theaters worldwide.

Chuck Nicklin about to dive from *Red Sea Diver 1* as the
IMAX camera system is lowered into the water.

Ambassador
Samuel Lewis
diving.

15

My Friend, the Ambassador

At historic peace talks or at sea, Sam dove right in

US ambassador to Israel, Samuel W. Lewis, heading out for a dive trip.

Operating a diving business in such a beautiful area, I met scores of fascinating people and forged lifelong friendships with some of them. At the top of the list was Ambassador Samuel W. Lewis and his wife, Sallie.

Sam, as we affectionately called him, served as US ambassador to Israel from 1977 to 1985, a period highlighted by the Israel-Egypt accords. Sam was an integral member of what became known as the "Peacemakers," the American diplomatic team that helped bring about the first peace treaty between Israel and an Arab nation.

Before taking up his post in Israel, Sam received some excellent advice. His good friend Ambassador Nicholas (Nick) Veliotes, finishing his tour as deputy chief of mission at the embassy in Tel Aviv, suggested that Sam pursue a hobby that would let him escape the stresses of Middle East politics and diplomacy. Nick had been one of my students and dived frequently at our new base in Sharm. He recommended that Sam contact me after settling into his new job.

It was not unusual to find a contingent of American diplomats and their families diving with us in Sharm during the 1970s. I looked forward to their visits because many had become friends and they came bearing gifts: Fritos, beef jerky, Milky Ways and Pepsi. The US Embassy had an amazing post exchange (PX) — a store that sold goods to both military personnel and authorized civilians — and was a gold mine for my longing for American junk food.

Shortly after Sam arrived, he invited Sharon and I to dinner at his official residence. We took our one-month-old daughter, Daria, the third of our four kids. The atmosphere was so informal that by the end of the evening, we were all sitting on their living room rug as I regaled our hosts with stories of Sinai and diving in the Red Sea. When Sam asked if I could give him private diving lessons in the residence's pool, I immediately said, "Sure, it would be my honor." And so began a forty-year friendship.

Over the eight years he served in Israel — one of the longest tenures for an American ambassador — Sam became the most popular diplomat in the country. He and Sallie were down to earth and loved to laugh. Sam quickly took to diving and escaped with us at every free opportunity.

On one trip, after coming up from a dive at Jackson Reef in the Straits of Tiran, Sam was excitedly telling me about a close encounter with a hammerhead shark when the skipper called me into the cabin. He told me that the Israeli prime minister's office had contacted the dive center looking for the ambassador on an urgent matter. I arranged a patch-up call from the boat to Menachem Begin's secretary and cleared the cabin so Sam and the prime minister could converse privately. One never knows what to expect on a dive boat.

Just months after Sam assumed his post, Egyptian President Anwar Sadat made his historic visit to Israel. For the first time, a prominent Arab leader was prepared to discuss a peace treaty with Israel. Sadat addressed the Israeli Parliament and, most importantly, the Israeli people. His visit to Israel would lead to the 1979 Egypt-Israel peace treaty.

The ambassador diving with our son Nadav.

With the treaty leading to Israel's agreed withdrawal from Sinai (in 1982), we had to move our home and business out of Sharm. Before we left, Sam came down for one last diving holiday. He had one request: He wanted to see a manta ray, the one large fish he had not encountered in his eight years of diving with us. On the last dive of the trip, at Ras Um Sid, we were hanging out in the shallows for a decompression stop. Suddenly, I saw Sam's face light up and he pointed over my shoulder. I spun around to face a beautiful manta. It was heading right in our direction as if answering Sam's wish. As the winged giant gracefully swam past us, Sam finned over to me and we danced an underwater waltz.

As Sam's tenure was ending, he and Sallie were invited to many going away parties. He turned all but one down: the one with his diving buddies. Sharon and I hosted the party at our home. Graphic artist Shlomo Cohen created a parting gift, a facsimile cover of *Time* magazine with Sam on it. Mike Burstyn, a famous American/Israeli entertainer, wrote and sang a number for the occasion, "Sam, Sam Diving Man." The ambassador loved it.

From the start of the peace process, Sam promised me that he would do everything in his power to impress upon all involved the importance of nature conservation and accessible water sports tourism in Sinai. He lived up to that vow.

Later in his career, Sam served as an assistant secretary of state under President Bill Clinton and as president of the US Institute of Peace. In 2014, I was honored to speak about our friendship at his memorial service in Washington, DC.

In an oral history collected by the Library of Congress, Sam shared his thoughts about his term as ambassador to Israel:

> "Diving permitted me to live through eight years in Israel; I would not have been able to last that long without it. The opportunity to slip away every two or three months to enjoy a few days of diving made the rest of the time bearable; when you dive, you forget everything else. Divers don't discuss politics; they barely know who the Prime Minister is and know little about his views. They discuss diving and fish, a great change for anyone in a pressure cooker such as Israel."

LEFT: Graphic artist Shlomo Cohen's parting gift to Sam.

RIGHT: Sam and Sallie Lewis enjoying a holiday with us.

Sam's dream manta showed up on his last Red Sea dive.

The ambassador (center) became part of my extended family.

Diver beside the propeller.

16

A Shipwreck to Call Our Own

Discovery turns rumors into reality

Arriving at Shaab Mahmoud reef, Gulf of Suez.

In the wake of the 1977 blockbuster movie *The Deep*, shipwrecks were all the rage in diving tourism. While we couldn't provide movie stars such as Nick Nolte, Jacqueline Bisset or Robert Shaw, we hoped at least to attract tourists with the prospect of a sunken treasure ship.

My imaginative friend Shlomo Cohen, author and graphic artist, cooked up a fantasy tale of a missing ship laden with gold bars sent to pay the Bedouin fighters serving with T.E. Lawrence (Lawrence of Arabia) during World War I against the Ottoman Turk forces who ruled the region.

We had only one problem: Over nearly a decade of diving in the Red Sea, we had yet to find a single diveable shipwreck. Not one! Sure, a few remnants of stranded ships sat high and dry atop the coral reefs, but none would sustain our homespun yarn.

Still, we would hint about such a ship when the opportunity presented itself. We would speak vaguely to visiting journalists, filmmakers and travel agents about a shipwreck we planned to explore. We promised the travel agents that we would let them know when the location was open for diving and told the journalists and filmmakers that we would give them the first shot at an exclusive article or movie.

Feeding the rumor mill was good for business. Several articles even appeared about the possibility of a Lawrence of Arabia treasure ship. But we knew we couldn't keep the fictional story going for too long. We needed a shipwreck and fast. Luckily, several Bedouin fishermen friends came to our aid with reports of a possible sighting.

They spoke of a rich fishing area in the Gulf of Suez where they could make out an unusually large shadow at the base of a reef when the sea was calm. Well off the Sinai shore, the reef rose out of nowhere.

The story rang true. Sunken ships, especially in tropical seas, spawn an ecosystem, starting with corals and sponges that attract nibbles from small fish that, in turn, are gobbled up by larger fish.

Bedouin fishermen over the reef.

"Smoke three cigarettes"

With GPS navigation for civilian boats like ours still years away, we had to settle on verbal instructions from the Bedouin fishermen. Cigarettes, rather than satellites, would guide us to our destination.

"Go around the corner at Ras Mohammed, head west into the Gulf of Suez, smoke three cigarettes, and in the distance you will see waves breaking on an offshore reef. Go to the southwestern tip of the reef, drop anchor and find the spot right below."

To say we were skeptical would be an understatement, but what did we have to lose by spending half a day exploring an unfamiliar reef? We were hosting an American diving group led by Carl Roessler, owner of See & Sea Travel. Over dinner, I asked Carl if his group would be interested in joining our search mission. Later that evening, after consulting with his clients, he said they were up for an adventure. The following day, we hoped to find something special.

When we rounded the point of Ras Mohammed, heading into the Gulf of Suez, I remembered the Bedouin fisherman's instructions to head west and smoke three cigarettes. Inconveniently, I was a pipe smoker and hated cigarettes, which left me trying to estimate how to convert cigarette time to pipe time. As a backup, I asked one of the crew members to smoke three cigarettes with twenty-minute breaks in between.

Sure enough, after he finished his third cigarette, we spotted waves breaking onto what appeared to be a coral reef far off the Sinai shore. We headed to the southwestern tip, where I suited up for a recon dive.

Shortly after hitting the water, I looked down and was surprised by the sight of a large, fractured ship resting upside-down on the seabed. It hosted a full house of aquatic life: huge groupers, barracudas, sharks, and masses of smaller reef fish of all shapes and colors swimming about the coral formations clinging to its steel hull. At last, we had found a proper sunken shipwreck in our corner of the Red Sea.

A sunken ship is a time capsule. As a student of archaeology, I was fascinated by the artifacts we pulled from the ship's holds, cabins and galley: porcelain plates, bowls, cups and glasses for hot and cold beverages, silverware, cooking utensils, rum kegs and wine bottles — some with corks still sealing the contents inside. We even found the kitchen sink, but sadly there was no treasure.

First sighting of the wreck lying upside down on the seafloor.

The wreck site located at Shaab Mahmoud in the Gulf of Suez, an
hour's cruise from our most famous dive site, Ras Mohammed.

It would take over a year and a BBC documentary film project to learn the name of the ship and its history. The first indication of a possible name was found on some of the dishes in the ships galley. The word "Dunraven" was embossed on them, even noting which section of the vessel they belonged to, like "Engineers" or "Cabin." Still these could have been borrowed from another ship. We took down a pneumatic grinder, powered by air from a dive tank, and chipped and ground away corals on the stern, where a vessel's name is normally found. One by one, the letters emerged, until they spelled out *Dunraven*. We had the name.

At that point, the BBC's research department kicked in, with producers back in the United Kingdom scouring the records of the British Admiralty and Lloyd's Register to learn as much as they could about a ship named *Dunraven*. Then the confusion kicked in — there were no less than three Dunravens on record!

So which *Dunraven* was ours? After spending days sifting through documents the BBC producers found the original ship's plans and solved the mystery. By a process of elimination, they were able to determine that our *Dunraven* actually sank on April 22, 1876, forty years before Lawrence's exploits during WWI. Our gold treasure theory was blown out of the water, so to speak, but at least we had determined which ship it was and learned its true history.

In spring 1876, the eighty-meter long British steamship *Dunraven* was bound for Liverpool with a cargo of wool and cotton from Bombay when it struck Shaab Mahmoud reef. A passing ship rescued the crew members before the *Dunraven* sank. Our Red Sea Divers discovered its undersea grave just over a century later.

The BBC documentary about the ship's discovery sparked widespread interest in the *Dunraven*. The wreck was also featured in leading international diving magazines. Nearly fifty years since its discovery, it remains a popular destination for diving tourists in the northern Red Sea. You can see the documentary *Mystery of the Red Sea Wreck* on my YouTube channel (as "Dunraven the World About Us").

My diving partners for the documentary were my partner Yossi Kivshany and his former commanding officer from the Israeli SEALs, Yohanan Spier, both very experienced combat and search and recovery divers. Yohanan after his navy service operated a marine salvage business and brought all the necessary tools we needed for the operation. The fourth member was Shlomo Cohen, charged with capturing our experience with his art skills.

With the BBC film project *Mystery of the Red Sea Wreck* (from left):
US Ambassador Samuel Lewis, director Eli Cohen (stretching out behind),
myself, underwater cameraman Chuck Nicklin and producer Dan Arazi.

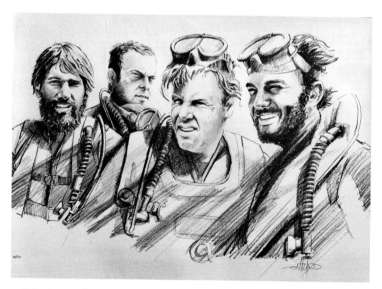

Principals of the documentary: Myself, Shlomo Cohen, Yohanan
Spier and Yossi Kivshany. ILLUSTRATION: SHLOMO COHEN

LEFT: Some of the *Dunraven* bounty, including the kitchen sink.

AT RIGHT FROM TOP: Gravy boat, serving dish and torpedo
bottles used to store mineral or carbonated water.

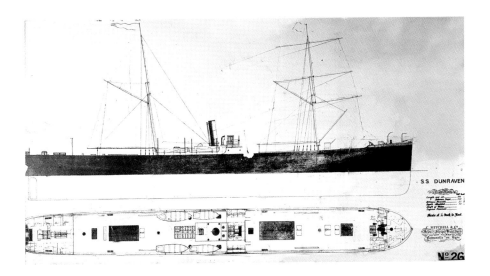

BBC producers unearthed original drawings of the *Dunraven*.

A near-fatal dive

During our dives to the *Dunraven*, we pushed the limits of our equipment and bodies. With sections of the ship lying at depths exceeding thirty meters, we faced the possibility of decompression issues. As an added safety measure, we planted backup diving tanks just outside the hull for emergencies and the lengthy decompression stops during ascents. Decompression sickness, commonly known as the bends, is an ever-present danger with deep dives. If a diver surfaces too quickly, skipping vital decompression stops, nitrogen bubbles can form in tissues and escape into the bloodstream. The potential consequences include intense pain, paralysis and even death.

On one particularly productive dive deep inside the wreck, I found myself running out of air. I headed for a large hole in the ship's side, which served as our main exit point and the location for an emergency backup tank, which I had placed there myself. But visibility was obscured by sand and silt inadvertently kicked up by the tourists from our boat.

I was close to panicking, which was not helpful. Still, I resisted the temptation to shoot twenty-five meters to the surface in an emergency ascent — a sure way to be stricken with the bends or a deadly air embolism. As my breathing became more labored, I noticed a stream of bubbles floating up through the silted water. I prayed their source was a leak from the emergency tank's regulator.

I followed the bubbles and found the tank. Grabbing onto it, I felt my way to the pressure hose, purged the regulator's second stage of seawater, inserted the mouthpiece and took the deepest breath of my life. I rested atop the tank for the next minute or two as my breathing returned to normal. I then replaced my empty tank with the full one so that I could make a twenty-minute decompression stop on my way up. It was a very close call.

Dunraven shipwreck. ILLUSTRATION: SHLOMO COHEN

Gorgonian fan coral.
PHOTO: DAVID DOUBILET

17

God's Other World

When film flounders, Navy comes to our rescue

Skin Diver magazine (February 1979 issue) featuring "Red Sea Odyssey."

When I made my first marketing trip to Europe and the United States in 1973, I tried to persuade the influential publisher of *Skin Diver Magazine*, Paul Tzimoulis, to do a spread on Red Sea Divers. But it was not until 1978 that we could attract enough advertising dollars to justify the project.

Paul assigned the story to the magazine's editor, Jack McKenney and his wife, Sari Gaines, who was also a model. As a bonus, Jack, an acclaimed underwater filmmaker, offered to do a promotional film simultaneously.

Jack and Sari found their diving paradise in the Straits of Tiran, the narrow shipping channel best known as a flash point for two wars between Israel and Egypt. In 1956 and 1967, the Egyptians blockaded the straits, which connect the Gulf of Aqaba to the Red Sea, thus cutting off the southern Israeli port of Eilat from the rest of the world. But strategic significance aside, the channel teems with marine life drawn to its four magnificent coral reefs — Gordon, Thomas, Woodhouse and Jackson — named for the British cartographers who first charted the area. These reefs lie midway between Tiran island and the Sinai shore. Jack opened his magazine story with a line that would reverberate throughout the diving world: "If I had to choose one place to spend the rest of my diving days, it would be the Tiran Straits."

During the shoot, the southern Sinai Bedouin sheikh of sheikhs, Abu Abdullah, chanced upon a scene of Jack filming Sari in a skimpy red bikini. Accustomed to seeing scantily clad tourists, the sheikh took no offense at her immodesty. On the contrary, without batting an eye, he offered to trade Jack five camels for his wife, in keeping with the currency of such arrangements locally. Jack and Sari took the proposition in good spirits but declined the offer. Sari was worth far more than that. The proud sheikh accepted rejection gracefully; he already had at least four wives.

We began exploring the *Dunraven* wreck just as Jack was wrapping up his cover story on Red Sea Divers. But our triumph might never have made it into the article — and accompanying promotional film — were it not for the help of our sometimes nemesis, the Israeli Navy.

Welcoming the opportunity to document the wreck, I agreed to Jack's request to take him and Sari out to the *Dunraven* in the days before they flew home. I also invited another well-known underwater filmmaker, Krov Menuhin, who was in Sharm at the time.

Early the following day, as we turned the corner at Ras Mohammed heading into the Gulf of Suez, our boat engine overheated and then died. Watching two significant, disappointed filmmakers tossed around in the swells, I could only pray that our engineer would work his magic. Just then, an Israeli Navy patrol boat appeared. Recognizing ours as a local dive boat, the crew pulled up and asked if there was a problem. I explained the situation and the skipper was kind enough to offer a tow to the nearest calm anchorage.

Jack McKenney filming with his state-of-the-art underwater cinema housing. Map showing the diving sites in the Straits of Tiran.

Jack shooting some images of Sari. The sheikh was impressed!

I was so desperate to get the filmmakers to the *Dunraven* that I had the nerve to ask the skipper if he wouldn't mind towing us to the wreck site instead. He tossed us a line to fasten to our bow. A half-hour later, we were moored in the shelter of Shaab Mahmoud reef, floating above the *Dunraven*.

Jack and Krov and their film crews dove in, wondering how long we could remain over the site. As they did so, a navy mechanic came aboard our dive boat and helped us repair the engine. Before the patrol boat took off, I invited the crew to dine at our dive club restaurant and promised an ample supply of Israeli Goldstar beer. We spent the rest of the day on the site, much to the appreciation of Jack and Krov, who obtained magnificent footage of the *Dunraven*.

Jack's article, "God's Other World: The Red Sea," appeared as the cover story of the February 1979 issue of *Skin Diver Magazine*. His film of the same name premiered at the 1979 Diving Equipment & Marketing Association (DEMA) expo, the most significant diving show in the world. Together, the coverage by *Skin Diver* and *National Geographic* did much to popularize diving tourism in Sinai and business at Red Sea Divers.

You can watch "God's Other World the Red Sea by Jack McKinney" on my YouTube channel.

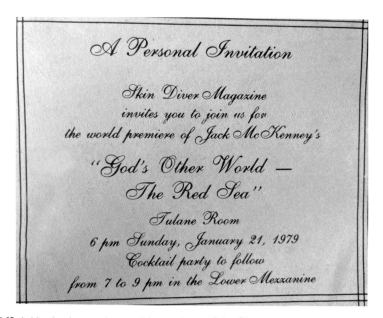

Official invitation to the world premiere of the film at the DEMA show 1979.

18

Finding Fortune in Misfortune

Cargo ships sound SOS, we seize opportunities

Loullia on Gordon reef.

For centuries, the Straits of Tiran — between the Gulf of Aqaba/Eilat and the Red Sea proper — have been synonymous with danger for mariners. Less than a kilometer wide at the narrowest point, the straits are lined with treacherous reefs that have claimed scores of ships over the centuries. Several stranded, disintegrating shipwrecks still dot the seascape.

As one of the few civilian operations with a fleet of boats, Red Sea Divers on occasion provided support services for salvage operations. Such jobs were action-packed and paid very well, so well that an insurance company executive half-jokingly suggested that I had managed to train the local ospreys to chew on the wires of light towers that demarcate one of the reefs. I could understand the company's wariness: Unscrupulous owners were known to wreck their boats for the insurance money.

The mysterious freighter

The fire-ravaged freighter sat at anchor at Ras Kanesa on the Gulf of Suez, where Netevei Neft, the Israeli national oil company, had a base of operations. We noticed it as we awaited the arrival of one of its vessels, the *Tom*, which we hoped to buy and convert into a dive boat. The company was selling off its equipment because Israel had committed to return oil fields in the Gulf of Suez as part of the peace accord with Egypt.

Our liaison with Netevei Neft told us that the company had towed the damaged freighter to a safe anchorage near their base after it caught fire in the gulf. We tried vainly to get a straight answer when we asked about its cargo.

We did not press the matter as our main interest was to inspect the *Tom*, which had just pulled alongside the jetty after a shuttle run to an oil rig. It was previously owned by Red Adair, the legendary oil rig firefighter from America. During the Yom Kippur War, Red and his twelve-meter boat were flown over to the Gulf of Suez in a giant transport plane to extinguish a raging fire on a Netevei Neft oil rig that had been hit by an errant Israeli Hawk missile. Afterward, the company bought the boat for more mundane duties like transporting rig crews and supplies.

The *Tom* had a large, flat back deck, well-suited for diving activities. There was a watertight cabin where passengers could stow their more delicate camera gear in the dry and divers could keep out of the chilly winds in the cooler months. After a test run, we left Ras Kanesa with our minds made up to buy the *Tom*, but I continued to wonder about what was in that freighter's hold.

A few weeks later, the damaged ship was towed into Na'ama Bay and anchored several hundred meters from our dive boats. Then, a strange thing happened: Large displays of La Vache Qui Rit (Laughing Cow) French cheese suddenly appeared in our local market.

The source? Our mystery ship. Enterprising Bedouin and Israelis had helped themselves to its cargo. Amazingly, the fire spared hundreds of kilograms of the creamy cheese. It took months to deplete the stock. Some residents overindulged and swore they never wanted to see a Laughing Cow package again.

Selling sand in Sinai

One morning a few months after the *Tom* joined our fleet, we picked up an emergency call on our marine-band radio from the *Niger Basin*, a cargo ship which was grounded on Gordon Reef at the southern entrance to the straits. We had a dozen Swedish divers aboard the *Tom* that day and I quickly rerouted the newest and fastest acquisition of our fleet. The vessel was capable of up to thirty-two knots at full throttle, and it sped off in the direction of the stranded ship. When asked about the sudden change of course, I told the Swedes, "We decided to upgrade your dive site."

As we approached, I radioed the *Niger Basin* to offer help. The captain responded by inviting me aboard. I had the dive master prepare the group to go under but told him to wait for my signal before jumping in. I did not want our Swedish guests to risk injury should there be any efforts to dislodge the freighter.

A member of the crew threw down a bosun ladder for me to climb the dozen meters to the deck. I was then escorted to the bridge, where I found the stressed-out captain. He took me to the chart room, indignantly pointing to the blue space on his map between Tiran island and the Sinai shore. Indeed, the coral reefs were not marked. The trouble was, he had a terrestrial map, little better than one you would get from the AAA. He should have had a maritime chart, which indicates reefs, shoals and other potential hazards.

When I offered him our services, he looked at our little dive boat moored aside his football field-length ship and asked how we thought we could help. Without hesitation (and with a fair amount of embellishment), I pointed to the Swedish divers on my boat and claimed them to be my team of expert underwater surveyors. I assured the captain they could take detailed photos of the damage that would satisfy his head office and insurers. After swiftly negotiating a price for the service, I gave the dive master the thumbs up.

In a matter of minutes, the Swedes, many with underwater cameras in hand, began their dive. The captain was impressed and I crossed my fingers that they would return with the promised pictures. As it happened, I did not need to fret.

While the dive crew went about its business, I chatted with the captain. He told me that his engineer had spotted a slight leak near the point of the collision and suggested plugging it with a special cement they had onboard. All they needed to make the cement was sand.

The group of Swedish divers on board *Tom*.

Tom tied up to the *Niger Basin*.

I scratched my head and said, "Sand? That is a problem!" At that moment, we were both staring at the shore of Sinai, one of the world's greatest sand-boxes. "What problem?" asked the incredulous captain.

Sinai sand, I explained, contained such a large concentration of salt that it was useless for cement. Okay, I was stretching things significantly when I added that construction crews had to rely on sand shipped from north Israel. I told him we had barrels of the special sand back at our diving center. The desperate captain bought my story and my sand.

The following day, we returned with a barrel of sand — freshly dug from the beach in front of our club. The *Niger Basin* crew made the cement and plugged the hole. With the help of high tide and no need for a tug, the ship backed off the reef. The outcome left everybody happy.

Sheikh Kabob

In 1980, *MV Lara*, a cargo vessel, was stranded on Jackson Reef in the Straits of Tiran. We picked up the distress call and helped rescue the crew. Later, I performed a diving survey for the insurer.

We were also contracted to watch over the vessel and assist the one crew member who remained on board to keep the ship's generators functioning. He told us the freezers in the hold contained large slabs of beef, lamb and pork. Pointing out that the generator would soon run out of diesel, I persuaded him to let us move the meat to commercial freezers in Sharm. A few days later, we received orders from the shipping company to transport the crewman from the ship to the airport, where he caught a flight home. No one ever questioned us about the cargo he left behind.

We sold the beef and lamb to a local butcher, who quickly took down his shop's kosher sign. For months, the people of Sharm enjoyed quality meat at bargain prices. We sold the pork to the foreign construction crews building a base for peacekeepers.

As previously mentioned, among the things we learned from the local Bedouin was how to make the most of whatever was available — an essential lesson for desert inhabitants.

The *MV Lara* when it went aground on Jackson Reef in 1980.

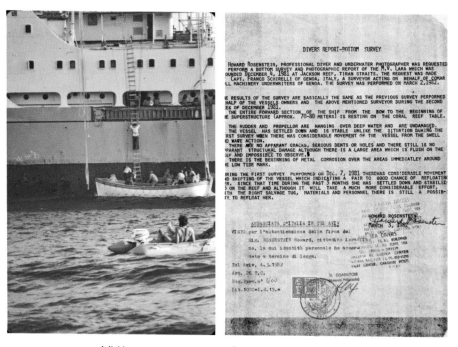

LEFT: *MV Lara* crew boarding lifeboat. **RIGHT:** Survey report.

19

Battling a Flood of Biblical Proportions

A lucky break saves our dive center

A tourist bus swept into the bay.

There is something very biblical about Sinai, even today. Guided by Moses, the children of Israel wandered for forty years in this rugged and barren wilderness. From the Suez Canal to the Israeli border, it stretches 240 kilometers at its widest point. From the Mediterranean Sea to its southern tip at Ras Mohammed on the Red Sea, the peninsula extends up to 385 kilometers. A vast desert plain in the north gives way to arid, granite mountains — the most famous of which is Mount Sinai. At its summit, the Bible tells us, Moses received the Ten Commandments; at its base, the Jewish people became a nation. Between the mountains are networks of intersecting wadis (dry riverbeds) and wherever water is found there are oases, often with Bedouin villages or encampments.

Besides miracles, Sinai has seen disasters. In late 1979, one of these inundated the coast of Na'ama Bay, threatening my life's work.

Sinai can experience rain from fall to spring, sometimes lasting a few days. Most alarming — and unpredictable — are bursts of heavy mountain rains that trigger flash floods. Such was the case in mid-October, when two successive storms soaked south Sinai. Massive rivers of water, boulders and debris rushed down the wadis, the already saturated desert soil cascading to the lowlands and on a direct path to Sharm and our location at Na'ama Bay.

Midnight call

Close to midnight Saturday October 20, I received a call from the civil administration warning me to secure our boats because of rough seas. I was at our home in Ofira taking care of our three young children while Sharon was away on a well-deserved vacation. Our house was built on a high bluff overlooking the Red Sea to the east and south and the mountains to the west and north. Thanks to its elevated position, it was not subject to flash floods. Until the call, I had been blissfully unaware of the tumult below.

The town of Ofira was built on a plateau overlooking the Red Sea.

After arranging for one of our crew to stay with the kids, I jumped into my jeep, picked up other staff members and headed to the diving center a few kilometers north at Na'ama Bay. Large pools of water made the road impassable for regular vehicles, which the police and army blocked from attempting to reach Na'ama. Fortunately, four-wheel drive vehicles were permitted and our jeep was up to the challenge, but it took twice as long as usual to get to the club. I had witnessed several instances of heavy rain in my years in the area, but nothing like this.

Usually dry wadis had been turned into rampaging rivers teeming with mud, boulders and uprooted trees. With power out and the moon covered by cloud, only flashes of lightning and the jeep's headlights illuminated the chaotic scene. Thunderclaps added to the drama. High winds sent Hawaii-sized waves crashing into the shore, colliding with the flood waters pouring down from the mountains.

Boats broke free from their moorings and were tossed about in the churning bay. Some grounded on the beach, where waves pummeled them to bits, our glass bottom boat included. Our small boat dock — the first in Na'ama Bay and proudly built with our own hands — had smashed up against boulders along the shore. Our crew — consisting of Bedouin, Israelis and Europeans — plowed an inflatable motorboat through the pounding waves to our two dive boats, which somehow had remained afloat at anchorage.

Running on adrenaline, we managed to steer the boats beyond the rough seas along the shore to calmer waters outside the bay. We rode out the storm until dawn, listening to the marine band radio as everyone checked in with each other. When an American colleague, a veteran sailboat operator, radioed that she was alone in her vessel and feared capsizing, we sent out a crew member in one of our inflatables to serve as her deckhand.

A bus was swept into the bay's shallow waters. Miraculously, all of its passengers were safely evacuated. Many parked vehicles were stranded in pools of rainwater and some washed into the bay. Bungalows, trailers and other light structures suffered severe water damage. One civilian official was electrocuted when he stepped into a pool of water strewn with downed power lines. In a communications bunker at the Air Force base just north of the bay, a young servicewoman drowned by her switchboard. Many young people camping on the beach lost all their possessions as they clung for dear life to elevated structures. Some Bedouin caught unawares along the shore or out in fishing boats were lost at sea. To this day, no one knows the storm's full toll.

The storm left the bay's normally aquamarine waters chocolate-colored and the shore littered with battered dive boats.

Bedouin women carting off the remains of boats to be used as firewood.

Our destroyed glass bottom boat.

The path of the 1979 flood.

Center's narrow escape

By morning, the storm had passed, but not before the flood waters had swamped the lower floors of the Marina Sharm Hotel next door, sending guests fleeing to the rooftop. The diving center itself escaped severe damage thanks to one of the many breaks turbulent waters had punched into the bay's pedestrian promenade, which had initially functioned as a retaining wall. One such gap, just twenty meters from the center, diverted flood waters into the sea. Even though Red Sea Divers was relatively unscathed, we were in no position to resume operations. Across the bay, a torrent smacked into our local competitor, the Aquamarine diving center. Repairing the damage took months.

Air Force helicopters and spotter planes launched search and rescue missions. Lt. General Rafael Eitan, chief of staff of the Israel Defense Forces, flew in to oversee the recovery operations personally.

It was days before electricity and clean running water were restored. Diving was out of the question as soil, debris and muck had turned the Red Sea chocolate brown. Reptiles commonly found only in the mountains floated in the bay or lay dead on the beach. The flood washed out stretches of the coastal road from Sharm to Eilat. Fortunately, Sharm's airstrip was spared. Military and civilian planes flew in essential supplies and evacuated stranded tourists, many with just the clothes on their backs.

After a massive month-long cleanup effort, services were mostly restored and diving tourism gradually returned to southern Sinai. Still, some roads remained unsafe and some buildings were too damaged for occupancy. The greatest danger came from old land mines washed down the wadis. A few landed in civilian areas, where ordinance experts detonated them. Meteorologists declared the storm the most violent and destructive to hit the Sharm region. If ever some scribe were to write an epilogue to the Bible, the Great Sinai Flood of 1979 would indeed be included — Noah or no Noah.

20

Birth of Diving Diplomacy

Red Sea explorers forge partnerships for peace

Meeting with Egyptian officials in Sharm to discuss the
future of Red Sea diving tourism and conservation.

In 1971, the US Table Tennis team became the first American delegation to visit Beijing since 1949, ushering in a thaw in US-Chinese relations. Through their shared interest in ping-pong, the two nations took the first steps toward building trust and seeing one another as people rather than faceless enemies.

I hoped that through diving diplomacy, I could foster personal relationships between Israelis and Egyptians in the wake of the 1979 peace treaty. I also had a personal stake: The accord called for Israel to make a phased withdrawal from Sinai over the next three years. While I was excited about the prospect of peace, I was worried about the fate of my dive center in Sharm, not to mention the life Sharon and I had created for our growing family there. Moreover, I was concerned about preserving Sinai's coral reefs, particularly Ras Mohammed.

Diving diplomacy was a sideshow to the main event, but I take pride in my persistence in navigating perhaps the trickiest waters of my career. I did so as part of a group of Red Sea diving pioneers and explorers who worked together to transform a historic war zone into an international tourism destination. We pushed to protect one of the world's most treasured marine environments and make it accessible to all. The experience was as frustrating as it was gratifying.

My three-year peace odyssey took me to Cairo three times, where I met with top Egyptian officials. It also took me to Jerusalem, where I was part of a group from Sharm who met with Israeli Prime Minister Menachem Begin. It had its farcical moments, such as when I joined a ragtag flotilla of Sharm settlers in a brief blockade of the Straits of Tiran; and its anxious ones, such as when a retired Israeli general and I were relaxing in a Cairo sauna when two other generals stepped in, both Egyptian.

Sadat meets the Shark Lady

The credit goes to Dr. Eugenie Clark for kicking off diving diplomacy. As I've already mentioned, Genie was known worldwide as the Shark Lady because of her pioneering research into the ocean's apex predators. She was also a bestselling author and expert marine life contributor to *National Geographic* magazine. Her connection with Anwar Sadat came through his son, Gamal, an enthusiastic diver whom she met at a photo contest in Cairo in December 1979. She did not initially realize who Gamal was, but then he invited her to his home, the presidential palace. As Genie raved about the wonders of diving at Ras Mohammed, Gamal interrupted, "You have to tell my father about this." He then left the room and returned with the president. The elder Sadat extended his hand to Genie and said, "You mean to tell me that I own the most beautiful reef in the world?"

Genie, who had learned basic Arabic while working on her doctorate in Egypt in 1951, regaled President Sadat with stories of dives off Sinai. When she told him she was about to return to Ras Mohammed, he offered to put two of his cars at her service and arranged for several marine scientists to accompany her. That night, with childlike excitement, she called to ask for my help organizing an Israeli contingent of scientists and environmentalists to meet her party.

I contacted retired Admiral Yochai Ben-Nun, a former commander of the Israeli Navy. During the War of Independence, Yochai led the commando raid that sank the Egyptian flagship *Emir Farouk*, the wreckage of which I helped discover in 1972 (see *Chapter 5*). Yochai, who had since become director of one of Israel's largest oceanographic research centers, agreed to send a top scientist to participate in the Egyptian-Israeli meetings.

On a December afternoon in 1979, I stood at the temporary border that ran from El Arish on the Mediterranean coast south to the southern tip of Sinai, established as part of Israel's phased withdrawal of the peninsula. Illuminated by the sun setting over the mountains, Sadat's Land Rovers approached with Genie and the Egyptian delegation. We ushered the group over the border, and, to the best of my knowledge it was the first time Egyptian scientists officially met with their Israeli counterparts — introduced by the amazing Genie.

The following day, I gave the delegation a tour of Ras Mohammed, which Israel had established as Sinai's first marine nature reserve nearly a decade before. While none of the Egyptians donned scuba gear themselves, they were impressed by the rave reviews given by diving tourists they met at the site. They learned from the Israeli scientists and conservationists all that had been done to protect the reefs.

The Egyptians' visit was captured on film by a CBS news crew. I had tipped off correspondent Bob Simon, who was in Sharm covering the peace process and Israel's pending withdrawal from Sinai, and who also happened to be my diving student. Simon reported on our efforts to preserve Ras Mohammed and its marine life. He also included interviews with Genie and her *National Geographic* team of David and Anne Doubilet, who were doing an article on sharks for the magazine. The more publicity, the better. You can see the resulting report, "CBS News Bob Simon with National Geographic in the Red Sea — Save the Sharks" on my YouTube channel.

Dr. Eugenie Clark (in the red jacket) leads a delegation
of Egyptian scientists over the interim border.

Genie's trip opened the door for me to contact the Sadat family. I wrote letters to the president's wife, Jehan, and their son, Gamal, to encourage their support in preserving Ras Mohammed as a diving destination. "[I]t is our most sincere dream that this area, along with any other nature reserve areas along these shores, will continue to be protected for the Egyptian people and the entire nature-loving people of the world," I wrote in my letter to Mrs. Sadat. I offered to host both on a tour of Ras Mohammed.

The Egyptian scientists' visit to Sharm lifted our hopes for future cooperation, only to have them dashed a month later when Egypt abruptly denied us access to the Ras Mohammed dive sites, now under its sovereignty. The crown jewel of the Red Sea was just four-hundred meters away, on the other side of the interim border. I felt like Moses: The promised land within sight but out of reach.

A disaster in the making

Matters went from bad to worse on April 1, 1980, when a Cypriot coastal freighter, the *Jolanda*, went aground at Ras Mohammed. The Israeli Navy tipped me off the morning of the accident. Standing in my front yard, I saw the stranded ship through my binoculars. I was anxious to get our dive team there to survey the damage and assess how it could be contained, but we first needed permission from the Egyptian authorities.

I called my friend and scuba diving student Samuel W. Lewis, the American ambassador to Israel. Whenever he could, Sam — as he asked us to call him — would break away from his responsibilities to dive with us in Sharm. In response to my request for help, he contacted the US embassy in Cairo. Within twenty-four hours, Egypt gave us the go-ahead. I gathered my team members and took a dive boat to the scene the next morning.

Reefs are built by colonies of soft and hard corals so fragile that they can break at the swipe of a diver's fin. Launched in 1964, the *Jolanda* was seventy-five meters long, eleven meters wide — a 1,153-ton freight ship complete with cargo — and it was wedged atop the northern coral island at Ras Mohammed's Shark Reef. Its captain compounded the damage when he tried to dislodge the vessel at high tide. Yet more corals were destroyed when the ship dropped its large anchor on the shallow seabed. *Jolanda* (pronounced Yolanda) came to rest on her port side in the shallows, but precariously positioned above a steep drop-off into the abyss. A bizarre array of cargo was strewn about the seabed: from containers filled with industrial plastic sheeting, to porcelain toilets, to a new BMW stuck head down between the islands.

When we arrived, a salvage vessel, the *Montagne*, had already dropped anchor atop a beautiful coral head that must have taken centuries to reach its size and majesty. Salvage operators are paid based on what they retrieve, a "no cure, no pay" agreement. As they let loose their chains and ropes, reef preservation is the farthest thing from their minds.

I photographed the scene above and below water, documenting the damage to the reef. Back at the dive center, I notified the American Embassy in Tel Aviv about the disaster in the making. My mission shifted from getting dive access to Ras Mohammed to saving the natural wonder.

Top US diplomats swung into action — Ambassador Lewis in Tel Aviv,

Ambassador Alfred "Roy" Atherton in Cairo and Ambassador to Jordan Nick Veliotes in Washington. Egypt halted the salvage operation within days.

The Swedish captain of the *Montagne*, a huge guy, was angered by our interference to the point of threatening my life. I first encountered him when I came up from my initial dive. Towering over me in an inflatable boat, he asked me what I was doing on *his* wreck. When he revved his outboard engine ominously in my direction, I quickly dove back down and navigated at depth toward the safety of our boat on the other side of the reef. At one point, the captain warned me of physical harm if I returned to the wreck site.

Surveying the damage done by the *Jolanda* wreck.

Salvage ship *Montagne* anchoring on the reef.

Jolanda anchor chain
sitting on the reef
at Ras Mohammed.
PHOTO: DAVID DOUBILET

After the Egyptian authorities expelled him from the *Jolanda* wreck site, the captain decided to see what he could salvage nearby from the *Dunraven*, the century-old sunken wreck we had discovered three years before. Leaving the *Montagne* anchored above, he dived into the wreck, never to be seen again. Ironically, the Israeli and Egyptian authorities enlisted me to search for his body just days after he had threatened my life. I combed *Dunraven*'s maze of silt-filled passageways, cabins, communal areas and cargo holds to no avail. Perhaps the captain had become stuck trying to squeeze through a narrow passage. Another possibility is that he had become disoriented in the upside-down ship and run out of air, trying to find his way out.

Over the next six years, Ras Mohammed absorbed the *Jolanda*, which essentially became an appendage to the reef that sank her. Coral colonies attached themselves to every available space on the submerged part of the wreck. Then, in 1986, a fierce storm dislodged the ship from its shallow perch, sending it 150 meters down to the base of Ras Mohammed. The wreck was not accessed again until technical divers reached it in 2005. Among the remnants in the shallows are a few of the toilets. This "rest stop" attracts divers eager to pose for underwater photos on the coral-encrusted thrones.

Once the *Jolanda* crisis was resolved, Egypt reimposed its restrictions on Ras Mohammed and we resumed our fight to have them lifted. We again turned to the good offices of ambassadors Lewis and Atherton. Prodded by the American diplomats, the Egyptians announced on May 15 that we could have sea, though not land, access to Ras Mohammed — and even that was restricted to the ten or so dive boats based in Sharm, half of which belonged to our Red Sea Divers fleet.

Instead of being able to come and go as effortlessly as we had in the past, we had to present a list of crew and guests, along with their passports, to an Israeli official in Sharm each day by a certain hour. The official would then drive to the temporary border at Ras Mohammed, where a tent had been set up for him to hand over the documents to his Egyptian counterpart. After reviewing the documents and stamping the passenger list, the Egyptians would issue one-day permits for diving the next day. The Egyptian officials had a famous expression "No problems, only procedures." Sometimes these procedures would mean no diving that day. Although the process was cumbersome, it marked the first time that I knew of that Israelis and Egyptians on either side of the border engaged in problem-solving as neighbors rather than enemies.

A brand-new BMW takes a dive at Ras Mohammed.

David Doubilet posing on a toilet.

Arriving at the interim border, where we had our diving visas stamped.

But to us, what mattered most was that we could again offer dive tours to Ras Mohammed and be able to monitor its preservation. We succeeded, for example, in helping to stop Egyptian fishermen from using dynamite to stun or kill schools of fish, devastating other marine life and the coral reefs in the process. We photographed fish and corals mutilated by explosions and shared the images with the Israeli and US authorities. They, in turn, pressed Egyptian officials who put an end to the practice.

LEFT: Egyptians fishing with explosives beside the remains of the
Jolanda at Ras Mohammed. RIGHT: Flying the Israeli and Egyptian
flags together as we switched countries during the diving day.

Dire straits

At the same time that Red Sea Divers was embroiled in disputes with Egyptians, we were waging a battle on the home front. While the Israeli government was mapping out plans to withdraw from Sinai, it dragged its feet on announcing compensation for settlers who would have to give up their homes and businesses.

We turned to a tactic Egypt had employed twice before, in 1956 and 1967. In the fall of 1979, Israeli residents of Sharm blockaded the Straits of Tiran — well, for a few madcap hours. And our closure didn't result in a war.

Unlike settlers of the Israeli-built town of Yamit in northern Sinai, we did not mount violent protests against the treaty with Egypt. Many of us felt making peace with our most dangerous enemy was worth the price, even if it included abandoning the lives we had established in Sinai. But with the final withdrawal two and a half years away, the government had yet to begin serious discussions with us about the financial implications. Meanwhile, compensation talks were well underway with northern Sinai settlements.

We felt ignored, perhaps because we had not kicked up a fuss. Among our questions: Would any of us be allowed to stay? Would evacuated residents and business owners be compensated for their business and personal relocation costs? Would housing be offered to the uprooted inside the pre-1967 borders?

The decision to block the straits came from an ad hoc meeting of Sharm residents. Before dawn on November 11, 1979, a ragtag armada of diving and fishing boats headed to the straits. We secured a rope that connected oil drums serving as floats to the light tower on Gordon Reef, with the intention of tying the other end to the Ras Nasrani light tower on the Sinai side of the straits. In theory, it seemed like a great idea. In reality, it turned into a comedy of errors. The rope, aside from being unwieldy, was too short. Strengthening winds whipped up the waters in the narrow passage to add to the mayhem. Many blockaders became seasick within minutes and some feared their boats would capsize. We were also spotted by an Israeli Air Force plane, which reported our suspicious activities to their base.

Realizing our scheme for the rope was doomed, we fell back on Plan B. One of the dive center vessels, trying out a new VHF marine band radio, sent out a message over the emergency radio channel 16. In several languages, it warned approaching ships not to enter the straits. A cargo ship heading down from the Jordanian port of Aqaba radioed back, asking what was going on. We responded that the straits were closed. The Israeli Navy picked up the exchange and notified us that we were violating international law. It dispatched a patrol boat to break up the demonstration. Overhead, a journalist was sending live reports to a popular Israeli radio station, having chartered a plane after we tipped the media off to the blockade.

We like to think we got Jerusalem's attention, though it would be well over a year before the government committed to a compensation package. At the very least, we showed that a $75 marine radio could close the Straits of Tiran. Unlike the Egyptians, we did not need cannons and warships.

A pint-sized power struggle

Yitzhak Navon, who served as Israel's fifth president, probably never forgot his family vacation in Sharm in 1981. During the visit, the local administration asked Red Sea Divers to entertain Navon, his wife, Ofira, and their two young children. We introduced them to the underwater wonders of the Red Sea with a slide show that included photos by David Doubilet, who happened to be in town to cover the Israeli withdrawal from Sinai and had amassed an outstanding collection of underwater photos.

We hosted the president on a cruise around Na'ama Bay the following day. Joining us was the famed naturalist Azaria Alon, one of the founders of the Society for the Protection of Nature in Israel. The sky was sunny and the sea was flat. We anchored in shallow water so the president could peer through crystal-clear waters at multicolored fish darting around a reef just below the surface.

As I explained the intricate symbiosis of marine life, I was interrupted by a commotion nearby on the deck. We were all startled to see a brawl had broken out between the president's six-year-old son, Erez and my five-year-old son, Nadav.

I ran over to stop the fight and keep the boys from rolling overboard. Once I managed to separate them, I asked Nadav what happened.

He said it began with Erez boasting about his father being the president. Nadav answered, "So what? My father is the captain, and the captain is the boss on this boat!"

Yitzhak Navon, the Israeli president, flanked by Azaria Alon and me.

President Navon with his son, Erez.

Diving a Ras Mohammed reef.

PHOTO: DAVID DOUBILET

21

Hans Hass

Diving with a pioneer

With Hans Hass at Ras Mohammed in 1980.

It's not often that one gets to meet a lifelong hero, let alone take them diving. I experienced this a few times, such as when I shared a speaking platform with Jacques Cousteau and, years later, dived with Apollo moon-walker Buzz Aldrin.

One of my early heroes, especially when I was a young diving instructor and travel entrepreneur, was Hans Hass, the Austrian diving pioneer and filmmaker. In 1939, Hass' first book of underwater photographs, *Diving to Adventure*, was published. He helped develop the Rollei Marin, one of the first commercially available underwater cameras. Hass produced 105 underwater films, many of which he appeared in alongside his wife, Lotte, herself an expert diver.

Hass' book, *Under the Red Sea*, was like a bible to me, and the film of the same name won first prize at the 1951 Venice Film Festival. At the time, his standing in the scuba diving world was equal to Cousteau's.

One can imagine the excitement at Red Sea Divers when we received word that he would be visiting Sharm and wanted to dive with us. We scrubbed down everything at the club, ensured all the gear was in perfect condition, and prepared our trusty, if not rusty, dive boat, *Red Sea Diver 2*, to host our famous guest.

I escorted Hans diving in the Straits of Tiran and Ras Mohammed. At sixty-one, he was a handsome and fit figure. With all his experience, he was still excited to return to the Red Sea. Before our dive, I was preparing the anchor when he came up to the bow and asked if he could cast it out into a sand patch himself. I nodded in the affirmative. He picked up the thirty-kilogram anchor and heaved it over the side like a paperweight. Once anchored, we geared up and I thought to myself, how many times had he done that in his forty-year diving career?

Once underwater, I had difficulty keeping up with him as he darted from one coral formation to another. He playfully swam after a large barracuda, pretending to film it even without his trusty Rollei Marin housing system in hand.

After the dive, he lamented that his wife couldn't make the trip as the Red Sea was one of her favorite diving locations.

He promised to send me a copy of his famous book about the Red Sea and he followed up on his promise once he got back home. *Under the Red Sea* was released in 1952 when I was just five years old.

In the 1950s and 1960s, Hans Hass and his wife, Lotte, were the poster couple of the diving world. PHOTOS: HANS HASS INSTITUTE HIST

Diving with barracuda. PHOTO: DAVID PILOSOF

Oceanic whitetip shark.

22

Heading to Cairo

Testing the water in an emerging peace process

Cairo on the Nile.

Hoping to continue diving tourism in Sinai after the Israeli withdrawal, in December 1980 I seized an opportunity to visit Egypt. One of our customers, a South African businessman, organized two days of meetings for me with Egyptian tourism officials and potential business partners.

At the time, there were no direct flights to or from Israel; Egypt still did not allow Israeli nationals into the country aside from official representatives involved in the peace process. I circumvented those barriers by flying to Cairo via Athens and using my American passport. I was too excited to think about the absurdity of spending an entire day traveling the 392 kilometers between Tel Aviv and Cairo. After the treaty was in place, direct flights would take just an hour and a half.

When I touched down in Cairo, I felt I had landed in an alternative universe. The airport PA system blared out Arabic announcements in contrast to the Hebrew I heard that morning at Ben Gurion airport. The arrival/departure boards listed flights to and from Damascus, Beirut, Baghdad, Sanaa and Riad — Arab capitals still officially at war with Israel.

At the immigration counter, I noticed images of President Anwar Sadat everywhere. Once Israel's great nemesis, Sadat had been the architect of the Yom Kippur War. After his courageous trip to Jerusalem in 1977 and his speech to the Knesset outlining his vision for peace, he became an overnight hero in Israel.

Americans were popular in Egypt at the time, the United States having replaced the Soviet Union as the superpower of choice and trusted mediator of the Middle East. But even with my US passport, I felt very Israeli in Cairo that day. After all, I had been living in Israel for ten years, spending eight of them in the Israeli-administered Sinai. It was hard to wrap my mind around, finding myself in the heart of the Arab world — in the capital of the nation that had been my country's greatest enemy. Yet, I was excited about exploring new possibilities for my business and tasting the early fruits of the peace process.

A driver/escort from my Egyptian host, the Marinjac Company, met me with a limo. At the first checkpoint, as we left the airport, I was jarred by the sight of police and soldiers armed with automatic weapons and mounted bayonets. There was no question that in Egypt, the military was in control.

Passing several checkpoints in the relatively short drive from the airport to my hotel, I was also struck by the masses of people on foot and in cars. Back then, Cairo's population was nearly twice that of all of Israel. Traffic was chaotic. Blaring horns were a constant soundtrack as we banged along the pot-holed roads. I timed the most prolonged honk-free period at eight seconds. When I arrived at my hotel, I could hardly hear myself think.

The hotel was in Heliopolis, an affluent suburb of Cairo and home to the Marinjac Company. After a fitful night's sleep, I had breakfast with my South African colleague to prepare for our meeting with Marinjac chairman Khalifa Zarrugh, an entrepreneur in exile from the regime of Libyan dictator Muammar Gaddafi. Khalifa was in his fifties and went by the moniker Haj, a title given to Muslims who have made the pilgrimage to Mecca.

Egyptian police and military were evident
everywhere, including outside museums.

A Cairo street scene: full of color, noise, pedestrians and vendors.

Marinjac, an international investment corporation, sought to benefit from the potential windfalls of the peace process. Haj Khalifa was interested in investing in hotels and tourism in the soon-to-be-repatriated Sinai, including my diving operation. We met in his spacious and elegant offices — a stark contrast to the World War I freight car where I started my business in Sharm seven years previous.

The center of attention

After the meeting, Haj invited my South African businessman friend and I to a dinner in our honor at his home with some of his top executives and government officials connected to banking and tourism. It was my first opportunity to meet Egyptians in a social setting and I wore my best-borrowed sports jacket and tie. The occasion differed significantly from the get-togethers I had attended in Europe and the States. Instead of starting off with small talk over drinks, we entered a large room where some thirty middle-aged and older men (no women) in dark suits sat in chairs against the walls under glistening chandeliers. All eyes turned to us as we entered the room. Did I ever feel like a fish out of water! Haj Khalifa rose and introduced us to his colleagues, who cordially shook our hands one by one. Once we had made the rounds, we sat next to our host until being called into dinner. I was to learn that this was a common protocol in Egypt for such social gatherings.

We had a follow-up meeting with the boss the following day. Then he assigned one of his top aides to introduce my colleague and I to Egyptian officials, including a government minister. My hosts always introduced me as an American expert and entrepreneur. My Israeli citizenship was never mentioned.

Questioned about the potential of water sports and diving tourism, I offered assurances that Sinai could become an international destination. I urged Egyptian investors to seize the chance to get in on the ground floor. At Haj Khalifa's request, I drafted a business plan for a diving resort, hotel, and fleets of vessels and vehicles to transport the guests to and from the diving sites. We kept in touch for a year afterward, but the plan never came to fruition.

***

The business side of the trip concluded, I traveled to the Red Sea port towns of Hurghada and Safaga for a first-hand look at Egypt's still-infant diving industry. I stayed at the Sheraton Hurghada, the nicest hotel in the area. I was struck by the plaque at the entrance: "This hotel was recently refurbished, having received extensive damage in the October War to Liberate Sinai," referring to the 1973 Yom Kippur War. I wondered if I was the first Israeli to stay there. I used my American passport to check-in.

The next day, I was the guest of the Club Med south of the city. The resort's French diving staff invited me to explore the waters off nearby Giftun island. They took me down seventy meters, way deeper than sport diving limits, but maybe that was a way to show off their skills. In return for their hospitality, I gave a slide show about diving in Sinai to hundreds of guests, staff and local officials. They greeted my talk with applause and many questions about Sinai's aquatic potential.

In Genie's footsteps

Before leaving Hurghada, I had one last stop to make, a nostalgic one. I owed it to my mentor Eugenie Clark to visit the research center where she had spent 1951 working on her doctorate under Professor Hamed Gohar, a renowned and trailblazing Egyptian oceanologist.

Perched beside the Red Sea, the center was locked and appeared abandoned. But as I was heading back to my taxi, a watchman appeared with a bunch of keys. He spoke broken English and I even poorer Arabic. I managed to convey that I wanted to see inside the place where my friend had lived and worked thirty years earlier. The watchman selected a key and unlocked the large front door.

With a creaking sound right out of a horror movie, the door opened to what appeared to be a lab entombed in time. Under the dust and tangled in cobwebs were jars of marine species in formaldehyde. I wondered if Genie had collected some herself. By the entrance stood a pair of large stuffed dugongs, native to the area and cousins to the Florida manatee. Thrilled to play the role of tour guide, the watchman showed me the biological differences between their genders.

The Marine Institute in Hurghada.

I left with mixed emotions, excited to have walked in the footsteps of Genie and Professor Gohar, but saddened that the research station had fallen into such a dilapidated state. In recent years, it has been renovated and much improved and now looks nothing like what I remember, judging by the photos I have seen.

***

I had to pinch myself each day during my week in Egypt as I thought about being in the nation that had fought four devastating wars with my adopted country. But despite that history, throughout the trip I never felt any element of threat or danger — in fact just the opposite. I felt intoxicated by the feeling that peace was becoming a reality and I could play a role in helping it along.

23

Begin, Sadat and the Maestro

Bernstein steals the show at Sharm summit

Maestro Leonard Bernstein diving with us in Sharm.

In June 1981, Sharm was at the center of twin surges in diplomacy and diving tourism. Perhaps because it was an election year in Israel, Prime Minister Menachem Begin invited his Egyptian counterpart, President Anwar Sadat, for a summit in our small town.

The diving season was in full swing, with visitors from around the world. *National Geographic* sent a team to cover the peace process and the impending Israeli handover of Sinai. Besides the diplomatic stars, Leonard Bernstein, the renowned conductor and composer — and frequent visitor to Red Sea Divers — was also in town.

Lenny conducting a Red Sea Symphony from our boat.

Lenny diving and dancing underwater.

When the summit was announced, the government declared that Sharm would be closed to tourism. All our Israeli and foreign guests would have to leave the day before it started. Shocked by the sudden disruption, not to mention the hit to our pocketbook, we immediately protested. I used all my contacts to reach Begin's military advisor, who at least managed to secure permission for the *National Geographic* team and Bernstein to remain.

Hundreds of journalists descended on Sharm, including crews from every major American and European television network. At the time, the town's tourist accommodations consisted of one hotel, one motel and five restaurants. Hearing that an American was operating a local diving center, correspondents interviewed me for local color. You can watch the reports on my YouTube channel: "ABC news covering the Sinai withdrawal 1981" and "NBC TV report on leaving the Sinai 1981."

The reporters went wild when they saw Bernstein having a beer with David Doubilet and me at the diving center bar. Bernstein lapped up all the attention with some fifteen journalists crowding around him.

David Doubilet and Leonard Bernstein at the diving center bar.

Sneaking past the Navy

The ABC News producer asked me to suggest stories they could cover while waiting for the summit. I told him I had heard that Israeli and Egyptian fishing boats, for the first time ever, were anchoring side by side just south of Sharm at Ras Mohammed during the snapper spawning season, when tens of thousands of the fish congregate there. The producer jumped at the idea and chartered our dive boat to film the event.

Bernstein insisted on accompanying us. The maestro was not easy to say no to and the ABC crew loved the idea of his coming along. Hearing of our plans, Doubilet and his wife, Anne, asked to join us, too. Hosting ABC News and *National Geographic* together was the ultimate media exposure for us.

The challenge now was how to sneak into an area that at the time was off-limits to tourist boats like ours. We decided our best course was to head northeast toward Tiran island and then loop southwest to Ras Mohammed. Navigating the moonless night with our running lights off was nerve-wracking, but we had to do it to avoid being spotted. Fortunately, our radar picked up dots along the coast indicating the fishing boats. The camera crews got their gear ready. I didn't have a clue what would happen next.

Moving in total darkness, we positioned the boat near the largest cluster of fishing vessels. Bernstein loved every minute of this experience so alien to his usual world of glitz and glitter. When we were fifty meters away, I allowed the film team to turn on its lights and clicked on our powerful searchlights. The entire area was lit up, exposing a small fleet of boats of assorted sizes.

We must have freaked out the Egyptian fishermen as they surely thought we wore the Israeli Navy launching a raid. With cameras running, we pulled up to the stern of the most prominent vessel. Its deck was strewn with bait and fish innards. The fishermen, dressed in jellabiyas, were listening to Arabic music blaring from a boombox. I cautioned everyone on our boat against boarding until one of our Arabic-speaking crew members asked for permission.

Imagine my surprise when Bernstein suddenly jumped from our bow onto the Egyptian boat's slippery aft deck and started mingling with the crew. Worried about how the fishermen would react to the sudden intrusion, I hopped over the railing to join him. I found him dancing with the biggest, swarthiest fisherman on the boat, a man nearly twice Bernstein's size. They were like whirling dervishes as they moved in sync to the Arab melodies. After a few minutes, the fisherman, who obviously had no clue that his dance partner was the most famous classical musician in the world, picked Bernstein up and kissed him on the cheek.

All the while, the television and magazine crews were filming and clicking away. Bernstein stole the show from the unprecedented gathering of Egyptian and Israeli vessels. His beaming face could have lit the way as we made the return trip back to Sharm. I would give anything to get my hands on this footage but to date, all my attempts have been to no avail.

An Egyptian fishing boat at Ras Mohammed during the snapper season.

My own "West Side Story"

I should not have been surprised by Bernstein's impetuosity. Years before, I was in Tel Aviv to meet the Doubilets for a *National Geographic* article when I heard that the conductor was in town. Shortly after I left a message for him at his hotel, he called back and asked if I could arrange a day of sailing out of the Tel Aviv marina, which he could see from his hotel room. I set something up for the next day and invited the Doubilets to join us. Unfortunately, the skipper canceled in the morning because of rough seas.

When I called Bernstein with the bad news, he said he was disappointed but still hoped to get down to Sharm after he finished his concert tour. As we were chatting, I mentioned it was my birthday. He invited the Doubilets and me to his penthouse suite to celebrate. He even ordered champagne and a birthday cake from room service. After salutations, blowing out the candles and a few glasses of the bubbly, Bernstein sat down at the grand piano the hotel had provided and asked me what I wanted to hear. I was dumbfounded: a command performance by the great maestro in my honor!

I struggled to think of something fitting, hoping to come up with the name of a piece he had played at one of his televised youth concerts I had loved watching as a child growing up in Los Angeles. In desperation, I blurted out "West Side Story."

Bernstein smiled, nodded and played a medley from my favorite musical. For an encore, he performed the Yiddish classic "Yidl mitn fidl" ("Yiddle with His Fiddle") and sang along in Yiddish, which he had learned as a child in the Boston area. When he finished, we gave him a laughter-filled standing ovation. He bowed as if he had just concluded a gala performance with the New York Philharmonic.

A summit without seats?

Back at the Sinai summit, Sadat and Begin were due to fly in the next day. As host of the *National Geographic* team, I was given press credentials and allowed to accompany the journalists to the airport for Sadat's arrival. The press was fenced off on an elevated platform, but I managed to get some great shots of Begin greeting Sadat. Afterward, we followed the motorcade into town. The summit site was a large, empty building next to our diving center. Locals had dubbed it the "White Elephant" since it was built for some project that had yet to materialize.

While Begin and Sadat were freshening up in their hotel rooms, an event organizer approached me in a panic. He told me no one had remembered to get furniture for the summit. I had my crew rush over chairs and tables from the diving center restaurant. They were in place just minutes before Begin and Sadat arrived.

Egyptian President Anwar Sadat (left) arrives in Sharm to meet
with Israeli Prime Minister Menachem Begin (right).

The meeting made headlines around the world, as had every step of the
peace process since Sadat's visit to Israel in 1977. Ringside as an official press
photographer, I could get candid shots. Watching the leaders take their seats,
I nervously chuckled at the thought of our flimsy bamboo chairs collapsing
and setting off an international incident.

Begin and Sadat pose for photographers at the summit
(chairs and tables courtesy of Red Sea Divers).

The army watching over Na'ama Bay.

A few hours later, the excitement was over. The leaders and their delegations flew back to their respective capitals of Cairo and Jerusalem; the media collected their gear and prepared their reports; and we resumed taking tourists diving in the Red Sea. In retrospect, I doubt the summit accomplished much beyond providing Begin an international photo op in advance of the Israeli elections later that month. Besides, Begin was likely preoccupied at the time with a secret operation that would take place a week later and 1,100 kilometers away: Israel's attack on Iraq's Osirak nuclear reactor.

A near collision of conductors

The day following the summit, Bernstein had to return to Tel Aviv and asked me to give him a lift to the airport. As we headed north, another jeep cut across our path from a side wadi. I had to swerve to avoid it. I was furious! Why did this jerk have to cut us off? Both vehicles stopped within centimeters of one another. Next thing I knew, Bernstein was jumping out of his seat and embracing the passenger from the other Jeep. I wondered what the hell was going on.

It turned out the passenger was Daniel Barenboim, another of the world's most famous musicians — at the time he was musical director of the Paris Philharmonic. Just think of what would have happened had our Jeeps collided. I envisioned the headline in the next day's *New York Times*: "Famous maestros killed in Sinai jeep crash." And I, as one of the drivers, would have become a footnote in history.

24

A Seat at the Table

My quest becomes official — and starts in a sauna

The Mena House Hotel (right), where the bilateral tourism talks were held.

For my next trip to Cairo, in late October 1981, I went not as an independent operator using an American passport but as a member of an Israeli delegation. By then, the Egyptians and Israelis were holding talks between teams representing corresponding government ministries. In recognition of the importance of diving tourism to Sinai, Israel's Ministry of Tourism invited The Israeli Diving Federation (TIDF) to participate as an advisor in the bilateral tourism talks. The federation selected its chairman, retired Brigadier General Shaul Givoli, to represent its activities and me to represent the dive travel industry.

With great excitement, we boarded a pair of chartered buses at Habima Square in Tel Aviv at 7 am for a direct trip to Cairo. The tourism minister, Avraham

Sharir, led the delegation, accompanied by officials and entrepreneurs interested in all aspects of tourism, including transportation, services and accommodation.

When we arrived at the temporary border crossing near El Arish on the Mediterranean coast of Sinai, we were met by the members of the Egyptian delegation. As official guests of the Egyptian government, we were whisked through the crossing. We then traveled another several hours to the Suez Canal. The scene of pitched battles during the 1973 Yom Kippur War, the canal zone was now bustling with people, vehicles and a menagerie of four-legged traffic, including donkeys and camels. We crossed the canal on a ferry and drove another two and a half hours to Cairo.

At the Cairo Hilton, the desk clerk winked at me as he handed over an envelope with my room key. His gesture puzzled me until I noticed the envelope was addressed to Mr. Mohamed Rosenstein. I guess that the clerk thought I was a fellow Muslim, even with my very un-Muslim last name! I have no idea how I ended up with it. Who knows? Maybe I was the victim of an Israeli colleague's mischievous sense of humor.

Exhausted and sore after the nine-plus hour bus ride, I took advantage of the hotel spa. As Shaul, the federation leader, was staying in the adjacent room, I invited him to join me. Shaul and I had been friends since his days in active service when he dived with my centers. As a general, he headed the army's educational and training programs. After Shaul retired from the military he became a high-ranking police officer. But there was nothing officious about him; he was friendly with a terrific sense of humor.

After checking into the spa, we changed into robes and hit the sauna. We reviewed the day's events there, but stuck to English to avoid drawing attention to ourselves. After a few minutes two tall Egyptian men, who appeared to be in their late fifties, walked in and took the bench opposite ours. While chatting, they welcomed us to Cairo and asked what had brought us to Egypt.

Hesitatingly, I said that we were members of a delegation to the peace negotiations between Egypt and Israel. I immediately regretted my honesty, knowing that not all Egyptians embraced President Sadat's initiative. But a few seconds later, the men smiled and said they supported the treaty. They said they had had enough of war between our nations. I breathed a sigh of hot sauna air in relief.

Then, one of the Egyptians extended his hand and introduced himself as General Ahmed and his friend as General Mohamed. I almost fainted.

On our first day in Cairo, we two Israelis found ourselves in a sauna with two Egyptian generals. I glanced at Shaul, who sensed my uncertainty but also my curiosity. He nodded toward me, which I took as a sign that it was okay to talk more about ourselves. I told the generals that I was Howard, a businessman from Sinai, and my colleague was Shaul, head of TIDF. I felt like the veritable ice had been broken in that very hot room; I savored the moment's symbolism: I was sitting with three generals, two Egyptians and the third Israeli. Less than a decade ago, they were bitter enemies. Today, they were sharing a sauna, each dressed in the same simple uniform of a towel across the lap. To all appearances, we were four ordinary guys schmoozing. But for me, it was a glimmer of the promise of peace. I had a sense that my battle-weary companions felt the same way.

Paying homage to Sadat

We arrived in Cairo when the treaty appeared in possible peril. Three weeks before, members of Islamic Jihad had assassinated President Sadat as he watched a parade commemorating Egyptian valor during the October 1973 war. Our first official stop was the site of Sadat's grave. He was buried at the pyramid-shaped Unknown Soldier Memorial, near the reviewing stand where he had been killed.

Five months before, I had photographed this great man, who was buoyant and beaming, as he arrived in Sharm El Sheikh for the summit with Prime Minister Begin. Would his successor, Hosni Mubarak, maintain the momentum toward peace? As to Sinai, would Mubarak share Sadat's commitment to protecting Ras Mohammed?

Egyptian Unknown Soldier Memorial, near where Sadat was assassinated on October 6, 1981, and where he was buried four days later.

Winning over the Egyptians

That first full day in Cairo was showtime for me, with day and evening presentations on my agenda. The first was at the internationally renowned Mena House Hotel, Sadat's designated place for discussions with Israeli leaders and the site of the bilateral tourism talks.

In my decade-long career, I had made numerous presentations on Red Sea diving all over the world. But this one was different. I felt the future of Sinai diving was at stake. Egypt had yet to divulge its plans for the region. Would it revert to its pre-1967 status as a virtual armed camp populated only by soldiers and Bedouin, or would its natural treasures be protected and available for all the world to see? I faced a challenging audience: government ministers, military leaders and senior bureaucrats. I doubted whether any of them had ever strapped on a scuba tank.

I wanted to stress two points: first, diving could be the backbone of a prosperous tourism industry in Sinai; and second, everything depended on Egypt retaining the stringent rules Israel enacted to protect the fragile ecology. I also recognized that I had to grab their attention from the start and keep them riveted. In other words, to influence them, I had to keep them entertained. After some thought, I came up with the opening: "Tourists will pay a lot of money to swim with sharks." That hooked them. I followed up with slides showing the extraordinary beauty of Sinai, from the mountains to the depths of the Red Sea.

Judging by the applause and questions the presentation was a success. So much so that officials from the Egyptian Ministry of Tourism invited me to a meeting the next day, at which they asked if I would be interested in continuing to run my diving center after the Israeli withdrawal. I was the only Israeli operator to receive such an invitation, most likely because of my US citizenship. They even presented me with a draft contract. But while I seriously considered the offer, I was not prepared to abandon the life I had made in Israel.

After the lecture, I met with US Ambassador Roy Atherton, a good friend of Ambassador Sam Lewis in Tel Aviv. Like Lewis, Atherton was a staunch backer of diving tourism. I thanked him for his role in stopping the salvage operation of the *Jolanda* wreck, and he pledged to provide whatever further support he could.

October 1981 tourism talks in Cairo (front row from left): Ali Jamal
Al-Nazer, Minister of Tourism, Egypt; his Israeli counterpart, Avraham
Sharir; and Rafi Farber, Director General, Israel Ministry of Tourism.

Ras Mohammed coral reef is among the richest and most beautiful in the world.

Peace gets personal

Ambassador Atherton had arranged for me to give a slide presentation that evening at the US Cultural Center in Cairo. This time, the audience was stacked in my favor. The center's staff went out of their way to invite Egypt's diving elite, tourism professionals and interested academics. I began my talk with an appeal to my fellow divers: "You are about to return to one of the most beautiful diving locations in the world. It is up to you to protect it against those who would exploit and even harm it."

At the presentation, I met Ayman Taher, a leading member of the small but dedicated Egyptian diving community. Ayman — whose father, Salah, was one of Egypt's most esteemed artists — peppered me with questions about Sinai and diving. He told me I was the first Israeli he had ever met. At his invitation, I had a lovely dinner with his family. For me, at least, peace was getting personal.

Sensing Ayman's sincere interest in Sinai, I promised to seek an official invitation for him to visit Sharm before the Israeli withdrawal the following April. I hoped the visit would help set the stage for a breakthrough in diving diplomacy.

Back in Israel, Sam was thrilled to hear about my successful trip to Egypt and soaked up every detail. True to his nature, the ambassador agreed to help arrange a trip to Sharm for Ayman.

Getting the Israeli officials on board went smoothly, but not the Egyptians. It was difficult for Egyptian nationals to obtain travel permits to Israel — forty years later, it is still hard. At my request, Sam contacted his counterparts in Egypt. They succeeded in getting a special permit for Ayman to visit accompanied by a staff member of the US Embassy in Cairo.

In March 1982, after coordinating our plans with the military, I arrived at the Israeli side of the temporary border just west of Ras Mohammed. After a few minutes of bureaucracy, the checkpoint barrier was raised and Ayman and his embassy escort walked through, diving gear and suitcases in hand. We embraced like childhood friends, climbed into my jeep, and off we went.

We dived together for a few days and Ayman charmed the invited group of elite Israeli divers. Sharon prepared a lovely home-cooked meal, capped by a chocolate cake with the flags of both countries and the inscription "Shalom" on it.

Stephanie Sagebiel, my liaison at the American Embassy in Cairo, sent me a cable after Ayman returned to Cairo. He relayed his excitement about the sites he had visited and how moved he was by our hospitality. She said that he had recommended to the minister of tourism that the Egyptians taking over Sharm's diving centers work with operations like mine during the transition period and possibly beyond. Sadly, that did not happen.

With Ayman Taher and Dr. Eugenie Clark at Ras Mohammed, where we promoted reef conservation efforts. PHOTO: AMOS NACHOUM

Going over maps with Egyptian and Israeli officers.

25

A Sneak Run Over the Border

Eluding Egyptians, we risk dives off their coast

George Balkyani at the wheel of the *Nirvana*.

As the diplomats ironed out the details of the peace treaty, we decided to get a jump on diving along Egypt's vast Red Sea coastline. Hundreds of miles of relatively unexplored coral reefs lay on the west side of the Gulf of Suez and further south all the way down to the Sudanese border.

Toward the end of 1981, an opportunity presented itself that I just could not pass up, though it entailed some risk. Among the boats we would charter to accommodate our diver overflow was the sailing yacht *Nirvana*, an eighteen-meter ketch commissioned in the 1920s for the Heinz family (of ketchup fame). The *Nirvana*'s owners, George Balkyani and his French-born wife, Elyan, made the classic yacht their home and a charter boat for companies like ours. Of Balkan heritage, George was raised in Italy and served as an officer in its navy during World War II. In their early sixties, they had aged well thanks to their nautical lifestyle. At some point, they became American citizens, but they were indeed citizens of the world. Multicultural and multi-lingual, they — and Sheba, their pet dachshund — were classy sea gypsies.

A classic two-masted sailboat, *Nirvana* was not designed for divers. Its narrow decks provided little room for storing and kitting up cumbersome gear. Made of teak, they did not bear up well under dinging from dive tanks and weight belts. We did our best to pad vulnerable spots, but the Balkyanis were rightfully disturbed whenever anything happened that might damage their pride and joy. They were good sports, though, especially after a few cocktails. The couple loved their Red Sea sojourns and became part of our extended family.

George suggested that we "sneak out" of Sharm one evening to try out diving along the Egyptian Red Sea coastal islands and reefs. So, under cloak of darkness, we eluded Israeli naval patrols and headed northeast toward Tiran island and Saudi Arabian waters. We then looped southwest toward Shadwan island, just off the Egyptian coast across the Gulf of Suez. The only vessels that we noticed were the freighter traffic traversing the Red Sea, appearing as distant blips on the *Nirvana*'s radar screen.

Shadwan island is about thirty-five kilometers northeast of the nearest Egyptian port city, Hurghada, and some fifty kilometers southwest of Sharm. With the prospect of peace in the air, we hoped we would be free to poke about the reefs of this largely uninhabited island.

Graveyard of ships

As we cruised along its northeast coast, we encountered rough seas whipped up by fierce winds in the Gulf of Suez. Just beyond the island's westernmost point, we noticed waves breaking on a barely submerged reef and sections of a rusting freighter. Based on our charts, we had come upon the submerged coral island of Abu Nuhas (Father of Copper). From later research, we learned that the reef system had claimed at least four ships, with one still partially visible after running up against a reef wall that year.

The shipwreck graveyard at Abu Nuhas off the western tip of
Shadwan island, with two vessels' remains still partially visible.

Egypt

Gulf of Suez

Shaab Ali

Abu
Nahas

Shadwan

SINAI

Red Sea

Ras
Mohammed

Sharm

Ofira

Aerial image of the area between Sharm El Sheikh and Shadwan island.

We geared up on the leeward side of the reef and then took our dinghy to the more exposed north side for an exploratory dive near the wreck. Within minutes, we stumbled onto what we later learned to be the British steam sailor *Carnatic*. In 1869, it had grounded on this spot, foundered and sunk. The Bombay-bound ship had moldered for 118 years in its watery grave, visited by just a handful of divers.

Diving the *Carnatic* was like swimming through a giant rib cage, as the ship's iron plates had long ago corroded away leaving a lattice-work of exposed deck beams. We found bottles and other artifacts similar to those we collected from the *Dunraven*, the 19th-century British wreck we had discovered a few years earlier almost directly east close to the Gulf of Suez's Sinai shore. Having been submerged in shallow waters penetrated by strong desert sunlight, the *Carnatic* was covered with hard and soft corals and teeming with marine life. It had become part of the reef that claimed it, the same fate as the *Dunraven*.

When sea conditions worsened, we scurried for shelter off the leeward side of Shadwan. After taking a few more dives, we dropped anchor at dusk in the protected shallow waters off the south coast. In the fading light, we spotted a few uniformed Egyptians in the distance hanging about an impressive stone lighthouse.

The wreck of the *Carnatic* (photo taken some years later).

LEFT: Exposed steel framework of the *Carnatic* after 160 years
under the Red Sea. **RIGHT**: A recovered wine bottle.

Shadwan lighthouse was the site of fierce fighting
during the War of Attrition in January 1970.

Just over a decade before, in January 1970, the site had been the scene of fierce fighting between Israel and Egypt during the War of Attrition, which followed the 1967 Six-Day War. Israeli commando units attacked the military base and destroyed its missile batteries. The lighthouse, severely damaged during the battle, was restored to full operation in 1987, six years after our visit.

It had been an adventurous twenty-four hours with the clandestine crossing into Egyptian waters across a choppy Gulf of Suez, and three dives on the wrecks interspersed with several exploratory snorkel recces of a shallow-water coral garden. After a tasty fish dinner prepared by master chef Elyan, and a few drinks, we headed below decks for a good night's sleep.

Suspicious soldiers, stormy seas

Outside of our protected anchorage, sea conditions remained rough, but time was running short before we were due back home the following day. When we noticed the Egyptian soldiers at the lighthouse pointing in our direction, we decided it was time to make a run for Sharm. We lashed down our sixteen scuba tanks and other gear, knowing that a loose cylinder in heavy seas could damage the yacht and cause someone serious injury.

Heavy waves crashed into the beam once we were out of sheltered waters. Despite our efforts to secure them, some scuba tanks banged against the woodwork. Even with all his years plying the world's oceans, Captain George looked ashen. Secured by safety lines attached to the railing, a crew member and I crawled about twelve meters along opposite sides of the raised cabin to reach the tanks at the bow. It took all our strength to steady them while securing them with extra lines.

Realizing that the boat could capsize if we plowed ahead, George wisely swung about and retreated to the calmer waters off Shadwan. We dropped anchor a bit west of our previous base, just out of view of the lighthouse guards.

George and Elyan were visibly shaken by the ordeal and the fear of losing their yacht. Indeed, all of us were rattled. We shared a bottle of Cutty Sark whiskey to settle our nerves and waited for nightfall, hoping the winds and waves would ease. By 10 pm the worst was over, so we raised anchor and headed across a much calmer sea toward Sharm. At first light, we arrived safe but exhausted in Na'ama Bay.

Nirvana heads into the rough waters of the Gulf of Suez.

Nirvana returning at sunrise to Na'ama Bay and flat calm seas.

26

The Troops Arrive

Enlisting the 82nd Airborne as eco-warriors

LEFT: El Al delivers to Sharm the first contingent of the MFO troops who would monitor the peace treaty. RIGHT: The 82nd Airborne meets one of the locals.

My efforts to protect the coral reefs and marine life off southern Sinai took me to Washington, DC, in late January 1982. I met with leaders of the Multinational Force and Observers (MFO), a special international military contingent established to monitor compliance with the Egypt-Israel peace treaty.

Beforehand, I had dinner with my old friend Eugenie Clark, professor of ichthyology at the University of Maryland, who was living in nearby Bethesda. Genie was anxious to hear what was happening in the Red Sea, where we had dived together so many times over the previous decade. Her eyes lit up when I told her that I would be pressing the MFO to add an environmental protection element to its mission. She immediately offered to accompany me to the meeting.

We arrived well-prepared for the MFO officials, me with a slide tray and projector in hand, Genie with her charm, prestige and knowledge. Our audience of military commanders and State Department officials listened as we explained the importance of protecting Sinai's natural resources.

I strongly urged the military to adopt a diver education program. At the end of the meeting, Lt. Colonel William Garrison, the soon-to-be base commander in Sharm, invited me to address his troops the day they landed in Sinai. I happily accepted.

Three months later, a contingent of 450 American 82nd Airborne Division paratroopers arrived in Sinai. They flew in from Fort Bragg, North Carolina, on an El Al Boeing 747, the first time such a big plane had landed in Sharm.

I was at the airport to welcome them and photograph their arrival. Wearing orange berets and camouflage fatigues, they carried M16 rifles and marched fifteen kilometers to their new base just south of Na'ama Bay. Colonel Garrison took the lead, with one of his legs in a cast. Just three weeks before, he had broken it in multiple places. Talk about being tough!

That night, as promised, Garrison had me address his troops. Despite the long flight and march, they were alert and excited about their new home and its beautiful surroundings. Introducing me, the colonel spoke of our meeting in Washington and the importance of protecting the fragile treasures of the Red Sea. As I walked to the stage, accompanied by my son Nadav, the troops started grunting at the top of their lungs. Startled, Nadav rushed into my arms. Evidently, grunting was this battalion's traditional way of showing appreciation.

Things quickly settled down. I gave a short speech welcoming the soldiers to Sharm, my home and workplace. Then, I presented an hour-long slide show about the area, its history, geography and, most importantly, precious environment. I urged them to take up diving and serve as volunteer rangers to protect the area's natural wonders. I also offered them an MFO discount at our bar, restaurant and diving center, a short hike over the hill from their base. I left hoping that I had recruited the troops to our cause.

The MFO did establish a recreational diving school. I often get comments on my social media posts from MFO veterans who tell me that Sharm was the highlight of their army careers. I can see why: It was like being at a resort, surrounded by beauty. Thankfully, there was little call for peacekeeping.

27

The Flag is Lowered for the Last Time

Even a meeting with Begin fails to stave off the inevitable

April 1982: The Israeli flag is lowered for the last time in Sharm El Sheikh.

The waning months of Israel's occupation of Sinai took me to Jerusalem as well as Cairo. With the fate of Ofira — the Israeli-built settlement in Sharm El Sheikh — still uncertain, I joined a delegation of residents for a meeting with Prime Minister Begin.

We were seated at a large rectangular table in the cabinet room. The air was tense. None of us had been in a situation like this; we had no idea what to expect. After waiting maybe five or ten minutes, the door to the prime minister's office opened and a small, bald, bespectacled man emerged. Despite his unimposing physical appearance, Begin exuded authority and confidence.

We all stood as he entered and sat in the only empty chair at the table, which happened to be next to me. He motioned for us to sit and warmly welcomed us to Jerusalem. Then he asked us to stand one by one and say a few words about what we did in Sinai. I was the last person called on since he started to his right and I was on his left.

As the only relatively recent immigrant in the group, I hoped my Hebrew would be up to the occasion. I told the prime minister that I owned a scuba diving center that brought many tourists to Sinai and was also involved in nature conservation. Holding up his hand, Begin stopped me in mid-sentence. "Are you the guy we must call every time we need to speak to Ambassador Lewis?" he asked. "The ambassador had told me that he loved diving in the Red Sea and only to call in an emergency." Everyone laughed.

Having disarmed us, Begin got down to business, calling the treaty a done deal and pitching it as an excellent opportunity for Israel. He said he had hoped to retain the coastal strip from Eilat to Sharm, but that proved impossible. We would all have to leave Sharm. In response to our questions, he said he had already appointed a committee to deal with the settlers' compensation matters and gave us his promise that we would be treated fairly. We talked for thirty to forty minutes, a long time for a meeting with the prime minister. While we did not get the firm commitments we had hoped for, Begin impressed us with his clear, unwavering message. He was determined to make peace with Egypt; nothing would stand in his way.

Na'ama Bay in 1982 at the time of Israel's withdrawal from Sinai.

Breakfast with George

George eyeballs a potential meal. PHOTO: LIONEL POZZOLI

Many of our regulars arrived for what they thought might be their last dive in Sharm. Among them was Marshall Michel, the air force attaché, who decided to spoil George, Ras Mohammed's resident and ever-popular Napoleon wrasse. Green and bump-headed, they are one of the larger fish species, but among several Napoleons who lived on the reef, George stood out as the biggest and most gregarious. Visiting divers fed him a steady diet of hard-boiled eggs sequestered from their hotel breakfast buffets. In principle, we opposed this as it interfered with their natural diet, but it was hard to police. Marshall's gourmet going-away present was a jar of pickled pigs' feet from the embassy PX. I watched him slip the jar into a clear bag and tuck it into his weight belt before descending. Unsure what he was up to, I followed. Encountering a slight current, Marshall clung to the mooring line as he sought out the famous wrasse. Unbeknown to him, George was waiting. He must have had a Pavlovian response to the sound of a boat, anticipating a handout as he lurked behind a large coral head.

Marshall paused to equalize the pressure in his ears. George, no doubt worried that a fellow Napoleon might show up and snatch *his* meal, furtively swam underneath the unwitting attaché. Sun rays penetrated the clear waters, reflecting off the jar and catching George's attention. Lightning-quick, he snatched it, bag and all, from Marshall's belt and sucked it into his gaping mouth.

Startled, Marshall flailed his arms. Worried he might bolt to the surface and risk an air embolism, I shot toward him. Seeing the bewilderment in his eyes, I pointed below to George, who was in the middle of his pigs' feet feast.

My concern shifted to the glass jar in George's stomach. Suddenly, I heard what sounded like a fish burp and saw George purse his huge lips. Then, wham! He upchucked the jar, followed by its cap, which floated gently down to the sea floor ten meters below.

Later, I admonished Marshall for being a naughty diver. Fortunately, George survived his bout of indigestion. But were he a Jewish or Muslim fish, he would now be in trouble with a higher authority for violating the taboo against eating pork!

Goodbye, Ofira

Israeli divers who came to say goodbye. At this stage no one really knew what was in store for the future of diving in Sinai.

By March 1982, Israeli civilians had started packing up to leave Sinai. We all had to be out by mid-April. Only Israeli officials and military could remain until April 25, when Egypt regained complete control of the region.

Some of us had been living in Ofira for a decade or more. Sharon and I supported the peace process, even though we were about to pay a high price both personally and professionally for the upcoming withdrawal from Sinai.

The entire community turned out for the tearful ceremony when we lowered the Israeli flag at our school for the last time. Just about everyone knew each other in this small, tight-knit settlement. Now, we were about to disperse all over Israel and beyond. Some families would break up under the strain and tension brought about by their relocation.

By then, Sharon and I lived in a tiny two-bedroom prefab house with a front-yard view of Ras Mohammed. We had three children: Ayelet, who was eight and among the first Israeli children in Sharm; Nadav, who was six; and Daria, who was four and a half. They had spent their infant years crawling on the beach and splashing in the bay's turquoise waters — or fast asleep in a shaded playpen next to the diving center. They were not happy about leaving, especially their school and Bedouin friends.

The Egyptian government established the Overseas Company to purchase and manage Israeli-owned tourism businesses including dive centers, motels and tourist villages like Neviot (Nuweiba) and DiZahav (Dahab). The Israeli government appointed a committee of army officers to assess the value of our businesses and negotiate with the Overseas Company. Fortunately, the Egyptians accepted the prices we requested, avoiding delays that no one wanted.

The 200th tank

The week before our departure, an Egyptian team visited the dive center to verify our inventory list, which we had prepared well in advance. The team's accountant was very thorough. We had listed two hundred diving tanks; he counted 199. We had to scramble to find one more — as if a single scuba tank might derail the peace treaty (or at least our sale of the diving center).

Thinking quickly, I ran to my office and retrieved a fire extinguisher. I placed it down with the other tanks. When the accountant asked why the 200th tank was red when all the others were yellow, I calmly explained that it was my personal tank. We were lucky he was not a diver.

After the inventory inspection, we sat down at one of the large tables in our patio restaurant for a signing ceremony. Noticing my partner Yossi peeling an apple with a fancy Swiss army knife, the chief Egyptian negotiator, Admiral Haluda, asked if the knife was part of the inventory. The query caught Yossi off guard and he did not know what to say. After I kicked his ankle under the table, he came up with the correct answer. He smiled at the admiral and nodded yes. The deal was done!

Bedouin staff from the diving center helped Sharon and me pack up our belongings and load them onto a truck bound for our new home in Israel.

They seemed as sad as we were about our leaving.

We almost forgot Saya, our shaggy rescue dog. With all the hustle and bustle of packing and getting the family to the airport for the flight to Tel Aviv, we left her behind! I returned to pick her up before heading to Israel in our beat-up Mercedes. It was my last departure from Israeli-administered Sinai, but not the last time I would be making the scenic drive along the Sinai coastal road.

The image of our family snorkeling that appeared in the April 1982 edition of *National Geographic*. PHOTO: DAVID DOUBILET

Time to pack up and leave Sharm.

28

Epilogue

Peace finally comes to Sinai

A memorial poster which was distributed at the time.

Although we had returned to Israel in April 1982, I still saw my future in Red Sea diving. I had been involved as a consultant to the peace deal's bilateral tourism agreements, ensuring Israeli divers would have access to the waters around Sinai reefs.

Less than a week after we moved into our new home in the small Mediterranean coastal village of Hofit, I flew to Cairo to sound out the Egyptians on ways I could stay in business. This time, I did not have to go via Athens. By then, Israel's national airline El Al had direct flights, which took an hour and a half from Tel Aviv. I no longer felt like a stranger on my third trip to Cairo. I had contacts in the American Embassy and among the

Egyptian public and private sectors.

To my delight, my old friend Genie Clark happened to be in town to talk with Egyptian officials about the nature reserve at Ras Mohammed, which she helped initiate in talks with Anwar Sadat in late 1979. She and her friend and benefactor Helen Vanderbilt were staying at the US Embassy guesthouse. Helen's family sponsored Genie's lab in Sarasota, Florida, which is today known as the Mote Marine Laboratory and Aquarium. The US ambassador, Roy Atherton, invited Genie, Helen and me to social events where I could reinforce my connections with Egyptian officials and others who would be open to my ideas about continuing to operate in the Red Sea.

Penetrating the Egyptian bureaucracy required vast reservoirs of patience. I spent many hours cooling my heels, waiting for meetings in smoke-filled offices. The Egyptians were generally courteous, although they tended to tell me what they thought I wanted to hear, which was usually the opposite of what transpired.

I also met with my diving friend Ayman Taher about a possible joint venture. As a member of a prominent family, Ayman helped me secure appointments with tourism officials, the new military governor of Sinai and well-placed leaders of the Egyptian diving community. They asked me about my experiences, the diving conditions around Sharm and the best sites to explore.

At that time, Sharm's tourist infrastructure amounted to little more than one hotel (the Israeli-built Marina Sharm, next door to my old Red Sea Divers Center); the Clifftop motel; a youth hostel; and a nature society field school with spartan accommodation. I proposed the idea of a fleet of floating hotels as an interim solution for accommodating visiting divers. I wanted to tap into the emerging market of liveaboard cruises, which were gaining popularity in the Caribbean and Australia.

While I did not make any deals during my five days in Cairo, I did obtain a provisional license to operate a dive boat in the Sinai region of the Egyptian Red Sea. The next challenge was finding suitable vessels to transform into floating hotels.

Ayman and I did not realize our hopes for a joint venture, but at my recommendation, he invested in a stretch of land in Sharm that turned into a commercial gold mine.

Dear Howard — Sunday April 18, 82

WELCOME
TO
CAIRO !!

Helen Vanderbilt & I are
staying at the Embassy
Guest House (around the corner
phone 22049.
Love
Genie

Welcome note from Genie Clark when I returned to Cairo.

A living legacy

The cooperative arrangements I had hoped for with Egyptian divers have yet to materialize. They instead relied on experts from Europe rather than Israel.

Thanks in part to compensation I received from the Israeli government, I purchased my first liveaboard diving yacht. Renaming it *Fantasea 1*, I launched Fantasea Cruises Ltd, toward the end of 1982. We offered diving excursions to the Egyptian Red Sea for the next fifteen years. In the early 1990s, we purchased the larger, more luxurious *Fantasea 2* and expanded operations to dive and explore the entire Red Sea and western Indian Ocean.

After the Sinai withdrawal, I hosted the *Geographic* team on these liveaboard diving yachts. For the November 1993 cover story, we dove along the entire Red Sea, starting in Eilat and heading south along Egypt, Sudan, Eritrea, Saudi Arabia, Yemen and Djibouti. Another great adventure, "Expedition to Aldabra," would take us to the Seychelles islands' massive atoll in the Indian Ocean. That story appeared in the March 1995 issue, the first time the magazine reported on the marine life at this World Heritage site.

Back in the Red Sea though, by the mid-1990s the Egyptians had built up their operations and began crowding us out. Ultimately, with high fees and red tape, the Egyptian authorities made it nearly impossible for foreign operators like me, despite my twenty-five-year history in the area.

What did diving diplomacy accomplish? It helped secure a provision in the peace treaty for a special visa to Sinai that allows thousands of Israelis to visit and dive there each year. Most importantly, it helped pave the way for Ras Mohammed to be declared Egypt's first national park and nature reserve.

Fantasea I liveaboard cruising the Red Sea.

Fantasea 2 liveaboard in the Seychelles.

Poster advertising Fantasea Cruises. ILLUSTRATION: SHLOMO COHEN

Epilogue to the epilogue

As I finish this memoir, war has once again engulfed our region. The hopes raised by the peace treaty of the late 1970s now seem imperiled, although Israel and Egypt are still collaborating in important ways.

In one of my early chapters, I wrote about diving the sunken ship *Emir Farouk* off the coast of Gaza. Today, the beach from which we launched our exploration is a battleground between Israeli and Hamas forces. Tensions are reverberating into the adjacent Sinai.

For the past fifty years, forty of them under Egyptian sovereignty, thousands of Israeli divers have been frequenting the dive sites in Sinai, only a few hours' drive from Tel Aviv and Jerusalem.

Since the October 2023 Hamas terror attacks, diving tourism from Israel to Sinai has stopped entirely. Many Israeli divers have sworn not to return after reading about Egyptian dive operators actively supporting the Hamas terrorists in their social media and public pronouncements.

We can only hope that once the war is over, confidence and trust will be restored and that the Sinai reefs will again welcome divers from all over the world, including Israel.

Acknowledgments

This memoir has been a half-century in the making. Its seed began in the 1970s when I was living in Sinai and operating one of the first diving operations in the Red Sea. Some of our guests suggested that I should take notes of this era of discovery and adventure. I am not one for writing a diary (I never even owned a diver's log), but I purchased a large notebook and every time something of interest occurred, I just wrote down a line in the hope I would remember the experience.

Luckily, I am an obsessive photographer and ever since my late teens I have more or less documented my life with a camera. That helped a lot with recalling the early years of my diving career. It also helped that my wife, Sharon, meticulously kept every article ever to appear about our dive operations in Sinai. Thank you, dear Sharon.

After shutting down my operations in the Red Sea and Indian Ocean in the late 1990s and moving on to other pursuits in the diving world, I stored away the tattered notebook and boxes of slides and articles. They probably wouldn't have seen the light of day without COVID-19 and the homebound exile it put us all in. Going crazy from inactivity and forced isolation, I decided to open Pandora's box of my early years in the diving business and begin to put form to the yellowing notes and rapidly deteriorating half-century-old color slides. With a trusty Epson slide scanner and pages of articles and notes to review, I worked two years to assemble this memoir.

A special note of thanks to so many who helped out, faithfully reading my missives and critiquing when I so often went off track. To my wife, Sharon, who let me drift off into dives of my youth and rarely asked me to resurface to attend to my regular household schedule and chores. To my memoir mentor Steve Maas, who mercilessly picked my brain to come up with long forgotten incidents and made an invaluable contribution with the editing and crafting of this memoir; my cousin Raima Evan, who kindly did initial editing in preparation for a respectable manuscript to send off to a publisher; and my old friend and diving colleague David Doubilet, undoubtedly the greatest underwater photographer of our generation, who kindly agreed to let me use his amazing images to help enhance the narrative. Finally, I thank my publisher, Alex Gibson, who so professionally steered a conglomeration of stories, maps and photographs to create this publication.

My sincere thanks to all of you — this narrative would never have surfaced without your kind support:

Steve Maas
Sylvia Earle
Raima Evan
Shlomo Cohen
David Pilosof
Viva Braun
Bernie Chowdhury
Bill Gleason
Rick Tegeler
Carl Roessler
David Doubilet
Anne Doubilet
Barbara and Marty Frank
Michael Fieldman
Dr. Michael Messer
Arnold Young
Dr. Irene Kitzman
Dr. Jose Castro

Leonie Barel
Marty Snyderman
Dr. Michael Jung
Hans Hass Institute
Sarit Zadok
Deb Castellana
Amos Nachoum
Bret Gilliam
Yoel Silverberg
George Linder
Oren Most
Danny Ratias
Kathy Sullivan
Noa Levin Rosenstein
Gan De Lange
Shay Ben Yitzchak
and Jonathan Flamm.

Index